LIFE UNDOCUMENTED

LIFE
UNDOCUMENTED

Latinx Youth Navigating Place and Belonging

EDELINA M. BURCIAGA

THE UNIVERSITY OF
ARIZONA PRESS
TUCSON

The University of Arizona Press
www.uapress.arizona.edu

We respectfully acknowledge the University of Arizona is on the land and territories of Indigenous peoples. Today, Arizona is home to twenty-two federally recognized tribes, with Tucson being home to the O'odham and the Yaqui. The University strives to build sustainable relationships with sovereign Native Nations and Indigenous communities through education offerings, partnerships, and community service.

ISBN-13: 978-0-8165-5304-4 (hardcover)
ISBN-13: 978-0-8165-5303-7 (paperback)
ISBN-13: 978-0-8165-5305-1 (ebook)

Cover design by Emily Weigel
Typeset by Sara Thaxton in 10.5/14 Warnock Pro with Neumatic Gothic and Helvetica Neue LT Std

Publication of this book is made possible in part by the proceeds of a permanent endowment created with the assistance of a Challenge Grant from the National Endowment for the Humanities, a federal agency.

Library of Congress Cataloging-in-Publication Data
Names: Burciaga, Edelina M., 1977– author
Title: Life undocumented : Latinx youth navigating place and belonging / Edelina M. Burciaga.
Description: Tucson : The University of Arizona Press, 2025. | Includes bibliographical references and index.
Identifiers: LCCN 2025003805 (print) | LCCN 2025003806 (ebook) | ISBN 9780816553044 hardcover | ISBN 9780816553037 paperback | ISBN 9780816553051 ebook
Subjects: LCSH: Children of noncitizens—California—Social conditions | Children of noncitizens—Georgia—Social conditions | Children of noncitizens—Education—California | Children of noncitizens—Education—Georgia | Latin Americans—United States—Social conditions | Noncitizens—United States—Social conditions | Illegal immigration—United States
Classification: LCC JV6255 .B87 20 (print) | LCC JV6255 (ebook) | DDC 305.9/0691073—dc23/eng/20250422
LC record available at https://lccn.loc.gov/2025003805
LC ebook record available at https://lccn.loc.gov/2025003806

Printed in the United States of America
♾ This paper meets the requirements of ANSI/NISO Z39.48-1992 (Permanence of Paper).

CONTENTS

ACKNOWLEDGMENTS

My greatest gratitude is to the undocumented young adults who allowed me to spend time with them, get to know them, and interview them. This book would not have been possible without their courage, generosity of spirit, and time. While I cannot share who they are, it is an honor to watch their lives unfold and to play a small part in capturing their story. I also want to acknowledge their parents and families, who have built their lives here and, as many young people conveyed, are the original dreamers.

Through this project, I had the opportunity to meet many wonderful people and advocates, and I would like to thank Laura Emiko Soltis, Claire Bolton, and Andy Kim for inviting me to join their efforts for educational equity in Georgia. Emiko, I am grateful for our continued connection and am thrilled when our paths cross. Thank you for the work you do for educational equity and social justice. I owe a special thank you to Adelina Nicholls for allowing me to make the Georgia Latino Alliance for Human Rights (GLAHR) my second home while I was in Atlanta, and to Monica Arboleda-Giraldo for welcoming me to GLAHR. Data collection for this project was challenging because I had to live apart from my almost two-year-old son. I owe a debt of gratitude to Wes Longhofer, Sonya Haw, and Harper for being my family while I lived in Atlanta. While in graduate school, I benefitted from research support from the Ford Foundation Dissertation Fellowship, the National Science

Foundation Dissertation Improvement Grant, the University of California Institute for Mexico and the United States (UC MEXUS), and the Society for the Study of Social Problems Racial/Ethnic Minority Graduate Fellowship.

The journey for this project to become a book was a long one, and along the way, I benefitted from the intellectual generosity, camaraderie, friendship, and care of many people. At UC Irvine, where I did my graduate work, I wish to thank Cynthia Feliciano, who initially challenged me to take on this project and whose guidance and feedback made it better. I also want to thank Jennifer Chacón, Ann Hironaka, Glenda Flores, and Rubén Rumbaut, who engaged with this project in its earliest iteration and whose insights significantly improved it. I am also grateful for my path crossing with Laura Enriquez while I was at UC Irvine. I also thank the members of "Cynthia's Clubhouse": Mariam Ashtiani, Matt Rafalow, and Yader Lanuza, and folks who were a part of the Race Research Work Group. These spaces were crucial to my growth as a scholar. I am grateful for the friendships that grew from these spaces during graduate school, including with Sheefteh Khalili, Yader Lanuza, Mariam Ashtiani, Jessica Kizer, Dana Nakano, and Kelly Ward.

I am incredibly grateful to the "ride or die" crew, Dana Nakano and Kelly Ward, for your weekly encouragement, the laughs, and the videos and memes that got me through moments of doubt, and whose friendship is invaluable. Irene Vega and I started graduate school together. While life ultimately took us along different paths, I am grateful for the time we had to write together and laugh together while living in Orange County, and for our enduring friendship as comadres in academia and motherhood.

When my family and I moved to Denver, I was welcomed by colleagues in the Department of Sociology at the University of Colorado Denver at the start of my academic career, including Stacey Bosick, Teresa Cooney, and Candan Duran-Aydintug, Keith Guzik, Adam Lippert, Carlos Reali, and Maren Scull. Jenny Vermilya, thank you for your support and lunches together. Thank you to my colleagues Jennifer Reich and Esther Sullivan for reading versions of the book proposal and the book, for checking in on me, and for the gentle encouragement to get it done.

While writing can feel like a solitary endeavor, I am thankful for my broader community at CU Denver. Faye Caronan is a trusted mentor, and I appreciate her wise counsel. I am grateful for Carrie Makerewicz's friendship and our time together at writing retreats and weekend Zoom sessions. Jennifer Camacho-Taylor has kept me grounded, and I cherish our coffee dates. Thank you to Sarah Hagelin, Meng Li, Krista Ranby, and Carole Woodall for the chance to discuss ideas in our writing group and for the happy hours and dinners. I am grateful for writing sessions with Sofia Chaparro, Boram Jeong, Lucinda Soltero-Gonzalez, Adriana Alvarez, Esther Sullivan, and Rachel Gross.

Beyond CU Denver, I treasure my *colegas* and *amigas* Lisa Martinez and Jazmin Muro, who offered encouragement, feedback, and solidarity. Colleagues in the Colorado Immigration Scholars Network and the Migrant Illegality Across Uneven Geographies workshops offered invaluable chapter feedback. I spent many writing sessions with Shalonda Kelly, who cheered me on with the book and my academic career. Natasha Howard, Jessica Kizer, and Carmen Johnston helped me keep an eye on the book while being mindful of my well-being. While they may not have been aware of the value of their support, I am grateful to the Ashley family, the Schade family, and the Hernandez family for having Noah over to hang out with your kids, which offered much-needed time to work on the book.

During the process of collecting data for this project, my dad, Paul Burciaga, lost his battle with pancreatic cancer. Words fail to adequately capture what his love and support meant to me. He had faith in me and this endeavor, which helped me at some of the most difficult times in this process. I am also grateful to my mom, Ruth Muñoz, who passed away in 2022. She was an incredible woman. As one of the first Latina staff members at Stanford University and eventually the assistant director for financial aid at Stanford Law School, she paved the way for me to enter academia. She helped care for my son as I finished graduate school and started my academic career. I will always be grateful for our time together. While I wish they could be here, they are always with me in my heart.

My family has always loved and supported me. I am grateful for my brother Raimundo Burciaga, my sister-in-law Angel Burciaga, and my beautiful nephew Eliades—your unwavering support anchors me. My Auntie Lydia and Uncle Manuel have been there every step of the way. Arthur Patterson has been there for us in countless ways. I am grateful to my in-laws, Pam and Greg Winters, for their steady support and love.

To my husband, Jamie: Thank you for being so supportive during our twenty years together. From encouraging my move away from practicing law to starting a PhD program, your steadfast belief in me gives me courage and confidence. Thank you for reminding me to strive for balance, to have fun, and to take care of myself. Your humor and love are a constant reminder that there is no other person in the world I would rather share my life with. Finally, to my son, Noah: You have grown with this project, and it is a joy to see the person you are becoming. You are bright, thoughtful, and persistent. Thank you for the lunch and movie breaks, silly jokes, and love. Every day, I am grateful that we took a leap of faith and brought you into the world.

LIFE UNDOCUMENTED

INTRODUCTION

Vanessa, an eighteen-year-old Deferred Action for Childhood Arrivals (DACA) recipient, greets me at the door to her home in the Atlanta metropolitan area. It is a mid-weekday morning, and as we sit at her family's dining room table, Vanessa and I discuss how she and her family ended up in the Atlanta area, migrating from Uruguay when Vanessa was six years old. Like many immigrant families, Vanessa's father was the first to migrate to the United States, and she, her mother, and her brother followed three months later, migrating on a ninety-day tourist visa. Vanessa started kindergarten at a local elementary school and quickly picked up English. Within that same school year, she moved to first grade and was identified as gifted, remaining in advanced courses through high school. When Vanessa entered high school in 2010, Barack Obama had been president for about two years. In her first year of high school, Vanessa wrote three essays about what it was like to be an undocumented immigrant living in Atlanta, Georgia. She shared that at the time, she was "really tired of people saying that I'm an alien, that I'm 'illegal,' that my parents are freeloaders, that I'm a freeloader. Because I'm not. I have struggled my whole life. We pay taxes. We do all of these things." She chose "the best essay," recorded herself reading it, and posted the video to YouTube. She was shocked when there were a thousand views in three days. The video also received the attention of her high school principal, who advised her to "lay low" until she turned eighteen, and Vanessa followed his advice, instead focusing on school and her goal of getting into college. Nevertheless, making the video did have one unintended benefit, as Vanessa was connected to a small group of other undocumented students in her high school. By her senior year, Vanessa knew that college would be expensive, but she did not know yet about "the ban" or the University System of Georgia Board of Regents Policies 4.1.6 and 4.3.4, which together effectively exclude undocumented students living in the state of Georgia from attending a public college. Although Vanessa graduated at the top of her high school class and would have been eligible for a state-funded scholarship to attend the University of Georgia, she instead found herself taking a "gap year" as she waited for admissions and funding decisions from out-of-state colleges—a prospect that caused anxiety because she played an important role in her family. She articulated her worries about the possibility of leaving for college in this way: "By me leaving, it's like who does my mom have to talk to during the day because, like, my brother doesn't speak well in Spanish, the kids [her younger siblings] don't speak very well in Spanish. Who is she going to talk to? And my dad, who is going to help him with work problems because he can't really, like, he can't express himself well, but you know, it's just [trails off] . . . Who is going to help my brother out with his homework, who is going to help my other [younger] brother with his homework?"

Vanessa's experience is emblematic of the experiences of many of the undocumented young people I interviewed in the Atlanta, Georgia, area. Like Vanessa, they were caught between wanting to realize their dreams of going to college close to home and being excluded by restrictive policies in the state. Because of the anti-immigrant context in the state of Georgia, these young people played an important role in their family's lives, helping them navigate daily life and long-term family goals, as Vanessa described. In sharp contrast, I met Miriam for our interview at her college campus in Southern California. Miriam, a nineteen-year-old DACA recipient, migrated to the United States when she was five years old on a tourist visa with her mother and two sisters. Like many undocumented immigrants, Miriam's family migrated to Southern California because they had family in the region. Miriam's father and mother had been living in the Los Angeles, California, area for a year while Miriam and her sisters stayed with their grandparents in Mexico. Miriam's mother returned to Mexico to bring Miriam and her sisters to California. Miriam recalled they made the trip around her fifth birthday and her mom promised a trip to Disneyland. While the possibility of visiting Disneyland was enticing, Miriam was most excited to see her dad and to have her family be together again. Miriam started kindergarten and, like Vanessa, she learned English quickly and excelled in school. But she also learned early on that she would need to advocate for her education, revealing the everyday complexities of race, immigration, and educational opportunity. During our interview, she shared,

> When I went to kindergarten, my teacher used to treat me like I didn't know anything. She would forget that I was even there. When they [the other students] would start learning the alphabet, they would change me to a class where a teacher actually spoke Spanish, so that I could learn the alphabet in Spanish, but I already knew it. So, it made me angry. I told my mom that I wanted her to go to the principal's office and tell them that I didn't want to be changed to a different classroom. She went, and they got into a fight, but at the end of the day, I was able to stay in my class. I started learning more English then.

By 2014, the same year Vanessa graduated from high school, Miriam was applying to colleges. Unlike Georgia, California has been at the forefront of educational access for undocumented students. California enacted Assembly Bill (AB) 540 in 2001, extending in-state tuition to eligible undocumented students. By 2013, as Miriam was aware, "The California Dream Act was already in order." The California Dream Act, AB 130 and AB 131, extended state and institutional financial aid to undocumented students who are ineligible for federal financial aid, making it slightly easier for undocumented students to pay for college. While Miriam confronted various barriers throughout college related to her legal status, she planned to graduate in three years and attend law school or graduate school. She shared, "I'm supposed to graduate in 2017. I plan my life a lot, so I have different plans: Plan A, Plan B, Plan C, and everything after that. Plan A would be to graduate from here [college] and go directly to New York University or Cornell to study international law. Maybe get a dual degree, a PhD. But if there's nothing I can do about the whole [immigration] reform, I'm probably going to end up going to

a law school here in California because I can practice here in California."
Although she was cautious about making declarations for her future because of her legal status and an uncertain policy context at the federal level, she was poised to experience the type of social mobility that the "American Dream" promises.

What explains the divergent educational pathways of these bright and ambitious young people? Both came to the United States as young children and were socialized in American schools. Both developed and nurtured college-going aspirations in high school, and both were academically equipped to attend college. Yet, their lives were headed in seemingly different directions. In this book, I trace the educational pathways and life-course trajectories of undocumented young adults in Los Angeles, California, and Atlanta, Georgia. While immigration law and policy are broadly regulated at the federal level, including who can enter with legal permission, states and localities have become increasingly important stakeholders in the immigration debate (Silver 2018; Garcia 2019). Nowhere is this more apparent than in the case of the metropolitan Los Angeles and Atlanta areas, two regions that have taken markedly different approaches to immigrant inclusion and exclusion, creating distinct legal ecologies for undocumented young adults.

In this book, I develop an understanding of place, or where one lives, as the site of experiences that are intimately shaped by law and policy. I examine how place shapes the lives of Latinx undocumented young adults like Vanessa and Miriam. Vanessa, and nearly all of the undocumented young adults I interviewed in the Atlanta area, aspired to go to college but, because of the restrictive policy context in the state, were not enrolled in college. Although many of the young people I interviewed in the Atlanta area had applied to colleges out of state, the prospect of leaving their families vulnerable in a hostile context weighed heavily on them. The undocumented young adults I interviewed in the Los Angeles region were enrolled in college or graduate school due in large part to accommodating college access laws in California. I extend this analysis to trace how other social forces, including the history of migration to these two regions, undocumented young adults' families, and other laws and policies influence where undocumented young adults are in life and how they envision their futures unfolding. In this book, I show how educational inclusion or exclusion had significant implications for other domains of undocumented young adults' lives, including their sense of identity and belonging, political participation, and orientation toward their futures. How undocumented young adults in two distinct contexts of reception made sense of the intersection between state laws and policies, dynamics at the federal level, *and* these other social forces as they navigated the transition out of high school and into early adulthood is the focus of this book.

The Legal Ecologies of Undocumented Young Adults

Vanessa and Miriam are members of the undocumented 1.5 generation, a group that includes undocumented immigrants who were brought to the United States as children. Many, although not all, have spent most of their lives here. In this way, they are like the immigrant, second-generation children of immigrants who are U.S. citizens. Yet, because they were not born in the United States and immigrated without legal authorization, their undocumented status has a profound impact on their lives. The day-to-day lives of undocumented young adults are shaped by layered and multiple contexts (Silver 2018), which I conceptualize as legal ecologies and theorize in the first chapter. The contemporary legal ecologies of undocumented young adults are the result of a decades-long approach to immigration that has moved away from integration and toward enforcement (Motomura 2014; Chen 2020). The modern-day enforcement and immigration policy regime in the United States is rooted in racist nativism, a unique form of racialized nationalism leading to a restrictionist approach to migration (Lippard 2011; Perez Huber et al. 2008). In the United States, immigration policy reflects a broader project of building a national identity by facilitating "the entry of immigrants deemed valuable while deterring those considered undesirable" (Zolberg 2006, 19). From the Naturalization Act of 1790 that limited naturalization to "free white persons of good character" to the Chinese Exclusion Act in 1882, suspending the immigration of Chinese laborers, race and national identity have long been intertwined. Historian Mae Ngai (2004) argues that the introduction of the 1924 Johnson-Reed Act marked the end of a laissez-faire era of European migration and introduced a new era of immigration restriction. Although the Immigration Act of 1965 lifted national-origin quotas, ending the "policy of admitting immigrants according to a hierarchy of racial desirability and establishing a system of formal equality in immigration" (Ngai 2004, 227), the newly introduced and evenly distributed quota of 20,000 immigrants per nation increased immigration from regions including Latin America, Asia, and Africa. It also contributed to the production of Mexican migrant illegality (DeGenova 2002; Ngai 2004). The last major comprehensive immigration reform, the Immigration Reform and Control Act of 1986 (IRCA), offered a pathway to citizenship for nearly three million undocumented immigrants living in the United States at the time (Motomura 2014). IRCA also ushered in an era of increasingly harsh enforcement, including employer sanctions, worksite raids, militarization of the U.S.-Mexico border, and increasingly punitive laws through the 1990s. Although immigration law is the purview of the federal government, in practice, laws and policies at the state, county, and city levels have a significant impact on the day-to-day lives of immigrants (Cebulko and Silver 2016; Silver 2018; Garcia 2019).

In the absence of comprehensive immigration reform, states and localities have taken up several measures that shape the lives of undocumented immigrants. At the same time, immigration patterns have restructured entire regions of the United States. Traditional immigrant gateways, like the Los Angeles region, have remained relatively stable regarding undocumented migration from Mexico and Central and South America, while the U.S. South, including the Atlanta region, saw rapid growth in this same population during the 1980s through the 2000s. However, demographic shifts alone do not explain the proliferation of restrictive policies in states like Georgia (Krishnan and Gulasekaram 2014). In addition to population shifts and the absence of comprehensive immigration reform, political context matters, with blue states enacting inclusive policies and red states enacting exclusionary policies, creating a variegated legal landscape (Krishnan and Gulasekaram 2014; Walker and Leitner 2011). From driver's licenses to college access, policies at the state level have created distinct legal ecologies for all undocumented immigrants, including undocumented young adults (Motomura 2014; Varsanyi 2010; Chavez and Provine 2009). For these reasons, California and Georgia offer insightful cases of the shifting dynamics of immigration law and policy at the federal, state, and local levels. Some states, like California, have enacted laws and policies that are inclusive and have eased daily life for undocumented immigrants. Other states, like Georgia, have enacted laws and policies that are exclusionary and make daily life difficult for undocumented immigrants. As Vanessa's and Miriam's narratives demonstrate, state laws, especially college access policies, have important implications for how undocumented young adults experience their present and envision their futures.

The legal ecologies of undocumented young adults have also been profoundly shaped by the DACA[1] program, which was introduced through an executive action by President Barack Obama in 2012. After nearly ten years of mobilization for the Development Relief and Education for Alien Minors (DREAM) Act, a legislative proposal that would have offered a pathway to citizenship, the Obama administration introduced DACA. Eligible DACA holders receive a two-year stay of deportation and legal permission to work in the United States with a work permit. At the program's start in 2012, estimates suggested that between 936,000 and 1.2 million undocumented young people were immediately eligible for DACA (Svajlenka and Singer 2013; Batalova et al. 2014). Two years after the introduction of the program in 2014, about 587,366 DACA applications had been approved (Batalova et al. 2014). Reflecting broader undocumented immigrant population dynamics, California was home to the largest share of the eligible population (371,000) in 2014, and by March 2014, nearly 183,000 undocumented young people had applied for DACA (Batalova et al. 2014). Georgia was seventh in the nation for eligible young people (39,000), and by 2014 nearly 21,000 young people across the state had applied (Batalova et al. 2014). Over the twelve years that DACA has existed, the number of DACA recipients nationally has been steady, with slight variation at the national and state levels. The DACA program's introduction through executive action as opposed to legislative reform has made the program vulnerable to rescission, which

---

1. To be eligible for DACA, undocumented immigrant youth had to meet certain criteria, including (1) having entered the United States before the age of sixteen; (2) being under the age of thirty-one at the time of application; (3) having a high school diploma or currently enrolled in school; (4) having continuously resided in the United States since June 2007; and (5) having been physically present in the United States at the time of the announcement. In addition, you must be at least fifteen years old to request DACA.

happened in 2017, and given ongoing legal struggles, the program has not been able to accept new applications regularly. As of June 2024, 535,030 eligible undocumented young people have received DACA nationally. There are 150,090 DACA recipients currently living in California, the state with the largest population of DACA recipients. Georgia is eighth in the country, with about 20,380 recipients calling the state home. As a growing body of research shows, state and local political contexts can mitigate or enhance the positive effects of the DACA program, underscoring the significance of place for the life course trajectories of undocumented young adults (Silver 2018; Burciaga and Malone 2021).

Place and the Lives of Undocumented Young Adults

Place is both a unique physical space and is given meaning through interpretation and experiences (Gieryn 2000). For the undocumented young people in this study, *place* was defined by where they physically grew up and lived, the Los Angeles and Atlanta metropolitan regions, and their experience of navigating their undocumented status in these regions. While laws and policies in each locale were key in shaping their day-to-day lives, other contextual dynamics also played a key role in their experience of place. Among these were the unique histories of migration to each of these regions and the historical and contemporary racial dynamics in each place.

During the 1990s, the United States experienced unprecedented growth in the immigrant population (Singer 2004). While many of these immigrants primarily settled in the six states with the largest immigrant populations—California, New York, Texas, Florida, New Jersey, and Illinois—the 1990s ushered in a shift in settlement patterns among immigrants. Growth in key industries, including construction and hospitality, drew immigrants to new destinations, including locales in the U.S. South, such as North Carolina and Georgia. These destinations became known as new immigrant gateways (Singer 2004; Singer et al. 2008). Unfolding alongside shifting trends in *which* states immigrants were settling in the 1990s was *where* they settled within metropolitan regions, with a significant shift toward settlement in suburban areas outside of large urban centers. Some of these urban centers, like Los Angeles and Atlanta, are physically characterized by their smaller central city hubs and sprawling suburban areas. This matters in part because the physical layout of a city shapes how immigrants navigate their day-to-day lives. Undocumented immigrants have unequal access to driver's licenses across states, and driving has become a source of vulnerability (Stuesse and Coleman 2014; Armenta and Alvarez 2017). In California, where all undocumented immigrants are eligible to receive a driver's license, participants discussed the relief they felt about their undocumented parents and loved ones being able to go to work or the store with less fear. In Georgia, where only DACA recipients are eligible for a driver's license, undocumented young adults shared their relief that they could help their families by taking siblings to school, driving their parents to work, or helping to run errands. In both Los Angeles and Atlanta, undocumented young adults discussed the stress that accompanied the seemingly mundane act of driving. Yet, in the Atlanta area, access to a driver's license created an added layer of responsibility that made it difficult for undocumented young adults to imagine leaving the area to attend college. This demonstrates the ways in which the physical layout of these cities intersected with state laws and local enforcement practices to create differentiated opportunities and obligations for undocumented young adults.

Beyond navigating the physical spaces of their communities, where undocumented young adults and their families settled significantly shaped their integration and mobility pathways. The process of immigrant integration is dynamic and evolves over the life course, particularly for immigrants who come to the United States as children (Portes and Rumbaut 2006; Gonzales 2016). It was in these communities where they went to school and developed friendships, key socializing experiences. For undocumented young adults in Los Angeles, a traditional immigrant gateway with a long history of Mexican migration, interviewees described communities where their undocumented status was inconspicuous because of the large Latinx immigrant population. This is not to say that participants did not perceive or experience anti-immigrant sentiment, especially those who were old enough to remember California's battle over Proposition 187. But Los Angeles's history as an immigrant gateway, particularly for undocumented Latinx immigrants, made the region seem more welcoming. Undocumented young adults in the Los Angeles area faced challenges in school, and yet they largely described schools that were prepared to work with immigrant students and had at least one bilingual, if not more, staff member or teacher. By high school, most participants had developed strategies for sharing their undocumented status with at least one trusted adult to navigate the college-going process. Unsurprisingly, in Atlanta, participants described entering schools that were unprepared to work with immigrant children. Many described not being able to share their undocumented status with friends or adults even through high school, cutting off important support mechanisms that are crucial to helping undocumented students navigate the path to college.

The final aspects of place that played a significant role in the experiences of undocumented young adults in Los Angeles and Atlanta were the unique racial histories and dynamics of each region. This book centers the experiences of Latinx undocumented young adults. While their legal status is a core aspect of their daily lives, their racial identity also matters. As sociologist Jennifer Jones observes, "Racial formation is deeply contextual and contingent" (2019, 7), and the local racial political context shapes the experiences of undocumented young adults. Under the first Trump administration, California became a symbol of a "sanctuary state," drawing the ire of the administration. In contrast, the Atlanta metropolitan area, the largest urban center in Georgia, increased local law enforcement cooperation with Immigration and Customs Enforcement (ICE), despite grassroots mobilization and a city climate that aims to be welcoming (Yee 2017). But this contemporary binary—one welcoming and one hostile—belies the complicated history of racial politics in each state and their broader regions. In fact, as this book reveals, hostile and welcoming contexts can co-exist in one place, and in the remainder of the book, I show how.

California was not always the welcoming place it is now. In the mid-1990s, California introduced Proposition 187, a state-level initiative that targeted undocumented immigrants and included harsh provisions affecting housing and schooling. The early 2010s witnessed a spate of laws that echoed the tenets of Proposition 187. While Arizona's Senate Bill (SB) 1070, referred to as a "show me your papers" law, received the lion's share of media attention, similar laws proposed in South Carolina, Alabama, and Georgia were much harsher. Like Proposition 187, the harshest provisions of these laws were unconstitutional and were struck down by the Supreme Court. While the Black-white binary is the predominant racial organizing logic in the South, agriculture in the region, including in Georgia, has long drawn Mexican immigrants (Weise 2015). These complicated racial histories speak to a broader question about the racialization of the Latinx population in the United States. The Latinx undocumented young people who participated in this study had a nuanced understanding of the racial dynamics in each of their regions. These dynamics shaped how they understood the relationship between racialization, citizenship, and belonging.

Belonging and the Emotional Lives of Undocumented Young Adults

Measures of immigrant incorporation examine how immigrants are integrating into society by focusing on key dimensions, including educational and labor market participation. While these measures are important for understanding the immigrant experience, equally important is understanding the affective or emotional dimensions of immigrant lives. The affective aspect of immigrant integration is often called a "sense of belonging" (Yuval-Davis 2006). In its most basic conceptual form, *belonging* means simply to be a part of. The complexities of the human experience, however, mean that people can be part of multiple groups and have varied and overlapping identifications and emotional attachments (Yuval-Davis 2006). For the undocumented young adults in this book, their identifications and emotional attachments were with both the United States and their country of birth, as well as their local regions. Additionally, their sense of belonging was partly informed by welcoming or exclusionary contexts at the local, state, and federal levels and their connections to their families and communities.

In both California and Georgia, undocumented young adults asserted belonging, actively resisting the exclusion imposed by formal legal status. Yet, local contexts played a key role in shaping the bounds of their belonging. In California, for example, undocumented young adults described how integrative educational policies at the state level signaled welcoming and aligned more closely with their sense of belonging. In contrast, in Georgia, undocumented young adults described a tension between their sense of belonging and the state's exclusionary educational policies. In both locales, however, undocumented young adults described an overarching sense of uncertainty and a forced orientation to the present. Planning for one's future is a key characteristic of the transition to adulthood. By high school, most young people in the United States are encouraged to contemplate how they see their future and what they want to be when they "grow up." Yet, implicit in this approach is an assumption of formal legal citizenship. The emergence of undocumented youth studies as a subfield of immigration research shows the ways in which navigating the transition to adulthood is complicated by legal status (Abrego 2006; Gonzales 2016; Enriquez 2020). As immigration scholars have noted, the inability to plan long-term is a key dimension of "illegality" and liminal legality, both uncertain or in-between legal statuses (DeGenova 2006; Menjivar 2006; Menjivar and Abrego 2011). Even with DACA, participants shared that they were only able to make plans in two-year increments, and the security associated with these plans was often contingent upon the political climate at the federal and state levels (Burciaga and Malone 2021; Silver 2018).

In a society like the United States that places a high value on college attendance as both a mechanism for social mobility and an indicator of a successful trajectory through adulthood, the systemic barriers undocumented young adults face navigating the pathway to and through college can be perceived as a barometer of one's success or failure. The participants in this study were acutely aware of the social value of a college education. While they appreciated that a college degree could help them reach their career and future goals, attending college had significant symbolic value as a way of honoring their parents' sacrifices. In both California and Georgia, participants described seeing how hard their parents worked, how they were exploited at times by unscrupulous employers, and how they experienced discrimination in daily life. These experiences underscored the commitment undocumented young adults felt to better their lives or to "keep the immigrant bargain." In his study of Mexican immigrants in New York City, Robert Smith (2006) introduces the concept of keeping the immigrant bargain. In this dynamic, children of immigrants push themselves academically to realize their parents' hopes and dreams for a better life when migrating to the United States. For undocumented immigrants, like the young people in this book, keeping the immigrant bargain presents an even greater challenge precisely because institutional access is limited. This made the barriers they faced in pursuing this goal much more emotionally difficult and impacted their sense of belonging. If belonging is understood as a two-way street, then understanding the emotional consequences of inclusionary and exclusionary laws and contexts is crucial for understanding the emotional lives and sense of belonging Latinx undocumented young adults experience.

The Study: Comparing Los Angeles and Atlanta

Immigration policy has long been the purview of the U.S. federal government. In practice, particularly in the last thirty years, states have been granted more liberty to enact policies that impact the daily lives of immigrants (Ramakrishnan and Gulasekaram 2014). Starting in the early 2000s, states and localities passed a flurry of laws that regulated daily life, particularly for undocumented immigrants, creating a variegated legal landscape (Walker and Leitner 2011). Over the course of the late 1990s and through the early 2000s, California became a more welcoming state, while states like Georgia became increasingly hostile toward immigrants. Even as Latinx undocumented immigrants were moving to new immigrant destinations, much of what we knew about the lives of undocumented young adults was based on foundational research conducted in California, with a focus on Southern California (Abrego 2006; Gonzales 2016; Enriquez 2020). These studies brought to light the challenges that undocumented young people faced navigating the transition to and through adulthood, including going to college, forming intimate relationships, and enduring the uncertainty associated with their legal status. I wondered what these challenges looked like for undocumented young people growing up and living outside of California (Cebulko 2014; Marrow 2011; Zuniga and Hernandez-Leon 2009).

After surveying the national immigration landscape, I purposefully chose Los Angeles and Atlanta—a traditional immigrant gateway and welcoming region and a new immigrant destination and hostile region—to examine the role of state laws and policies, as well as local dynamics, in shaping the life-course trajectory of Latinx undocumented young adults. As I discuss in depth in the next chapter, Los Angeles and Atlanta have distinct racialized histories and state and local policy dynamics. Yet, these two sites also share some key characteristics. Namely, they are sprawling metropolitan regions with vibrant immigrant communities. While immigration, especially by undocumented Latinx immigrants, has been happening in the Los Angeles area for quite some time, creating longstanding immigrant communities and support networks, I found that the Atlanta area also had immigrant enclaves and immigrant rights organizations that existed for the better part of twenty years. This book is based on comparative ethnographic fieldwork and seventy in-depth interviews with Latinx undocumented young adults in metropolitan Los Angeles, California, and Atlanta, Georgia. To be eligible for the study, participants had to be older than eighteen, be undocumented or DACAmented, and have grown up in and/or live in the Los Angeles or Atlanta metropolitan areas. I conducted six months of focused fieldwork between October 2014 and March 2015 in Atlanta. Fieldwork in the metropolitan Los Angeles area was ongoing between 2010 and 2016, with focused fieldwork for this study between April 2015 and October 2016. The open-ended interviews, which form the heart of the study, explored various topics, including young people's migration histories, childhood experiences, transitions out of high school, and perceptions and understanding of laws and policies that affected their daily lives and futures. During these conversations, Latinx undocumented young people revealed key insights into how they made meaning of navigating the transition to and through adulthood in two very different places.

I first embarked on this work in 2010 in Orange County, California, where I was in graduate school. An initial study of the activist experiences of undocumented young adults in Orange County and Los Angeles, California, helped me to establish ties. In the initial stages of my research and throughout my time as a researcher, my own personal identity as a third-plus-generation Latina and granddaughter of migrant farmworkers created a connection between myself and undocumented young people and Latinx allies in activist spaces. For many of the young people I got to know, I was one of a few Latinas they knew who had navigated the path to and through college, law school, and graduate school. While I shared a racial and ethnic identity with many participants, as I pursued this research, I began to see the unearned benefits of my own citizenship and how my own path was facilitated in important ways by having citizenship. As I progressed through graduate school, I nurtured and maintained relationships by becoming an active ally in the undocumented immigrant youth movement in Orange County. On a more practical level, before the passage of a driver's license law in California, I regularly volunteered to drive other members of an organization to statewide meetings or workshops that were held in Los Angeles or San Diego. Drawing from this experience, when I moved to Atlanta, I knew that establishing and nurturing ties with immigrant rights organizations would be crucial not only to the data collection process but also to developing a fuller picture of the undocumented immigrant experience in the region.

In the fall of 2014, I moved to Atlanta, where I spent the first month connecting with two immigrant rights organizations in the area. I initially volunteered with one organization as a grant writer, and with the other as a volunteer driver. I continued doing both for the remainder of my time in the area. Because of my experience with these organizations, I expanded the reach of my study to include folks who lived in Athens, Georgia, the home of the University of Georgia, and a key site for mobilization and action because undocumented students are banned from attending the flagship university. Cumulatively, my experiences as an active member and ally in organizations in the metropolitan Los Angeles and Atlanta areas helped me to complete the formal interviews that form the heart of this study. But the time I spent with undocumented youth and immigrant rights activists at meetings, work, meals, social events, and especially in the car, provided key insights that inform my claims. These "informal" interviews are also part of the corpus of data, along with field notes taken at community meetings and social movement events and actions. To understand the legal landscape of each site, I also engaged in an analysis of the historical and contemporary development of laws, policies, and regulations at the state, county, and city levels, supplementing with news articles as necessary to paint a more complete picture of the sociopolitical context. This data provides a rich picture of the daily lives and aspirations of Latinx undocumented young people in the Los Angeles, California, and Atlanta, Georgia, areas.

Overview of the Book

In the pages that follow, I trace the life-course trajectories, from childhood to early adulthood, of the undocumented young adults I got to know through this study. These trajectories are retrospective because I interviewed participants during early adulthood. I start in chapter 1 by analyzing the historical and legal landscapes of California and Georgia. These states are nested within a broader federal context that, for a long time, had been dominated by immigration federalism and preemption. I discuss how key legal changes in the early 2000s, both legislatively and judicially, set the stage for the fractured landscape of immigration policies and practices that currently shape the life-course trajectories of Latinx undocumented young adults. I situate the current legal landscape within the unique racial histories of these two regions and discuss how race, place, and the law intersect. The book follows a temporal trajectory, drawing from the accounts of Latinx undocumented young adults and how they developed an understanding of their legal status, the role of law in their everyday lives, and their prospects for social mobility, primarily by going to college.

In chapter 2, I compare the childhood experiences of undocumented young adults in Los Angeles and Atlanta. I find that the early life experiences of participants were not significantly shaped by their *own* undocumented status. Instead, as children, their lives were punctured by glimpses of "illegality" through the experiences of their undocumented parents. Participants' childhood experiences reveal the nuance and importance of place in shaping their early understandings of what it means to be undocumented, as young adults described observing their parents navigate the challenges of being undocumented and yet, despite legal barriers, building lives for their families. These formative experiences were important for shaping undocumented young adults' legal consciousness—how they internalize ideas about the law—but for many participants, they formed the foundation of their desire to attend college to better their own and their parents' lives.

In chapter 3, I focus on participants' high school experiences and ostensible transitions to college. As others have noted, it is during these years that undocumented young adults begin to realize the challenges and barriers they face on the road to college. The experiences of participants in Los Angeles and Atlanta were qualitatively different because of college access policies in each state. All participants from Southern California were either enrolled or had graduated from college. While in sharp contrast, only three participants in Atlanta were enrolled in college. In the Atlanta area, most participants were actively pursuing college. However, they had to navigate a host of factors, including the hostile climate in the region toward undocumented immigrants that left their parents and other family members vulnerable. The more inclusive environment in California and the Los Angeles region made it instrumentally easier for participants to attend college. Still, once in college, participants described experiencing a different form of educational exclusion.

Despite significant challenges and barriers, participants remained cautiously optimistic about their futures. The introduction of the DACA program provided some stability for participants in both Los Angeles and Atlanta. In chapter 4, I discuss how participants imagined their futures unfolding and how DACA shaped their sense of belonging. While uncertainty about legal access to residency or citizenship at the federal level pervaded the long-term plans of undocumented young adults in both places, they faced more immediate daily struggles, including how they saw themselves as part of the United States, the country they had lived in for most of their lives. Moving beyond the narrative of "Americanness," some undocumented young adults critiqued laws, policies, and systems that sought to deny their humanity. Yet, others embraced their sense of Americanness to explain why they felt compelled to remain in the United States. Both groups of young adults asserted their sense of belonging and yet drew from it very different definitions of what it means to be American. These ideas shaped if and how they saw their lives unfolding in the United States.

In chapter 5, I examine how Latinx undocumented young adults navigate engaging or avoiding participation in youth activism for immigrant rights. While some participants felt compelled to join the undocumented youth movement, others expressed reservations about the risks their involvement might present to their families. Engagement in activism was not neatly tied to locale—for example, less involvement in hostile Atlanta and more involvement in welcoming California—but instead reflected the complex intersection of local sociopolitical dynamics with family obligations and educational goals and/or realities. In this chapter, I also focus on a subset of participants in both Los Angeles and Atlanta who were actively challenging racist and nativist policies through activism. In both locales, there is a rich history of immigrant rights activism. I trace this history, connecting the vibrant undocumented youth movement to broader histories of Latinx immigrant activism and important legal and social changes. I examine how key institutions in both areas cultivated and sustained undocumented youth activism.

I conclude by tracing important judicial and legislative changes in the time that has passed since I initially started this study. In the wake of the election of Donald Trump as the 45th and 47th President of the United States, who ran both times on a nativist and anti-immigrant platform, welcoming states like California and hostile states like Georgia have become further polarized in their approach to undocumented immigrants. In both regions, ongoing judicial struggles over the DACA program underscore the importance of comprehensive immigration reform that provides a pathway to citizenship for Latinx undocumented young adults. I discuss the implications of the fractured legal landscape for Latinx undocumented young adults' sense of belonging and citizenship. I conclude by offering policy interventions that would work to incorporate undocumented young adults and their families and would strengthen communities in the process.

CHAPTER 1

THE LEGAL ECOLOGIES OF LATINX
UNDOCUMENTED YOUNG ADULTS

The influence of law is powerful not only in its presence but also in its absence. The last major comprehensive immigration reform regularizing the status of unauthorized immigrants was in 1986, with the passage of the Immigration Reform and Control Act (IRCA). IRCA adjusted the status of nearly three million undocumented immigrants but also ushered in an era of harsher border enforcement and a sanctions regime (Motomura 2014; Rodriquez et al.2010). In the time since the passage of IRCA, the undocumented immigrant population has grown to nearly eleven million, the result of a confluence of the United States's need for workers, increased border enforcement, and limited, if not nonexistent, pathways for legal migration (Motomura 2014; Pallares 2014). In addition, undocumented immigrants currently living in the United States are subject to various policies at the state and local levels that have created distinct political contexts, ranging from welcoming to hostile (Motomura 2014; Varsanyi 2010; Rodriguez 2008).

The increase in state and local immigration policies in the early to mid-2000s reflected a break from the long-held legal doctrine that "the power to regulate immigration is unquestionably a federal immigration power" (*De Canas v. Bica*, 1976, 354, as quoted in Rodriguez et al. 2010). These laws tended to proliferate in communities wrestling with rapid demographic shifts in their immigrant populations and were focused primarily, although not exclusively, on deterring undocumented immigrants from settling in these localities (Rodriguez et al. 2010). However, many policies during this time were also focused on integrating immigrants by expanding rights and benefits (Varsanyi 2010). The proliferation of restrictive policies not only signaled a devolution of immigration enforcement to states and localities but also reflected a "grassroots response to the presence (or potential presence) of undocumented immigrants" (Walker and Leitner 2011, 156). To understand the legal ecologies of undocumented young adults, it is crucial to understand how laws and policies intersect at the federal, state, and local levels to create a layered and varied sociolegal and political context for young people and their families (Silver 2018; Garcia 2019; Golash-Boza and Valdez 2018). The legal ecologies of undocumented young adults shaped their legal consciousness starting in childhood through early adulthood and, ultimately, their experiences of inclusion and exclusion in key dimensions of their lives, including their educational trajectories, their sense of identity and belonging, and their participation in activism.

In this chapter, I discuss the legal ecologies that Latinx undocumented young adults navigate. I start by comparing the immigration histories of metropolitan Los Angeles, a traditional immigrant gateway, and Atlanta, a new immigrant destination. While the labels "traditional immigrant gateway" and "new destination" are useful for measuring *recent* unauthorized Latinx migration to each region, these characterizations also obscure the complicated histories of Latinx communities in each of these cities and states. The broader racialized history of each region also informs its current approach to Latinx undocumented immigrants. Following the passage of IRCA in 1986, the federal immigration landscape shifted toward an enforcement and sanctions regime (Rodriguez et al. 2010). This turn toward punitive immigration laws, coupled with the absence of comprehensive immigration reform over the past forty years, has led to a fractured legal landscape at the state level, particularly in states that have experienced an influx of undocumented immigrants. I discuss some of the significant areas of law, both immigration-related and general, that signal whether a state is welcoming or hostile. Rather than focus exclusively on higher education laws and policies, I also examine other areas of law that shape the lives of Latinx undocumented young adults *and* their families in California and Georgia. As I discussed in the introduction, Latinx undocumented young adults' lives and experiences of illegality are fundamentally shaped by those of their families, creating another layer of contextual experience. This narrative thread is woven throughout young people's experiences in California and Georgia. Figure 1 captures the nested nature of the legal ecologies of undocumented young adults. Understanding these legal ecologies helps in identifying the multiple and, at times, competing social forces that shape the trajectory to and through adulthood for these undocumented young people. As sociologist Alexis Silver (2018) notes, the intersecting nature of federal and state laws and policies act like tectonic plates, shifting the metaphorical ground underneath undocumented young people's feet. I find that these shifts vary by where undocumented young people live and grow up, especially as state and local laws become increasingly crucial for navigating their day-to-day lives and, ultimately, shaping their aspirations and expectations.

In the chapters that follow, I analyze the experiences of Latinx undocumented young adults in California and Georgia within the framework of legal ecologies. I find that Latinx undocumented young adults envision their lives in relation to multiple contexts, including their families, state laws and policies, and the overarching federal context. Although

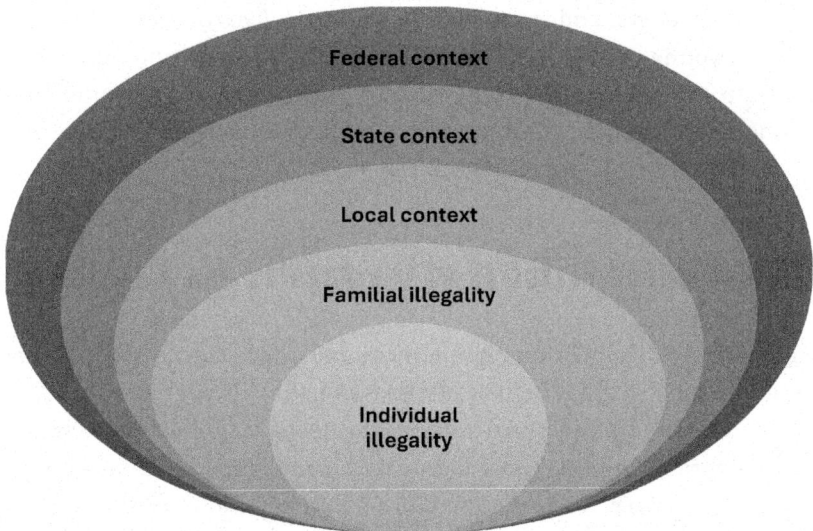

FIGURE 1 The Legal Ecologies of Undocumented Young Adults.

not captured in figure 1, the legal ecologies of Latinx undocumented young people exist within the broader social milieu of racist nativism and white supremacy, pervasive social forces that inform immigration policymaking over time, and lived experiences of racial discrimination and anti-immigrant hostility. In an era of increased criminalization of the broader undocumented immigrant population (Chacón 2012), undocumented children and youth are the only group in recent history to receive federal immigration relief through the Deferred Action for Childhood Arrivals (DACA) program. Although DACA has provided significant benefits to those who are DACA holders, the power of these benefits depends largely on state-level laws and policies. In this chapter, I examine a host of laws and policies that signal inclusion or, conversely, exclusion. These laws and policies have material consequences for the daily lives of undocumented immigrants but also carry symbolic meaning, providing insights into how Latinx undocumented young adults understand these shifting sociolegal contexts and their role in shaping their present and their future. By comparing the experiences of undocumented young adults in the Los Angeles, California, and Atlanta, Georgia regions, I find that many aspects of these young people's lives are similar, signaling the enduring power of federal immigration policy and the context of reception at the national level. Yet, this comparison reveals critical insights about how federal and state contexts shape the lives of Latinx undocumented young adults, and how they navigate the transition into adulthood. To understand the contemporary experience of undocumented young adults, though, it is important to unpack the history and legacy of the racialization of Latinxs in each region.

The Racialized Histories of Los Angeles and Atlanta

Beyond their divergent immigration law and policy contexts, California and Georgia also differ in their histories of Latinx immigration. California is considered a traditional immigrant gateway, a symbolic destination for immigrants, especially for Latinx undocumented immigrants (Gonzales 2016; Singer 2004). Of the 10.5 million unauthorized immigrants living in the United States, approximately 2.3 million live in California

(Perez et al. 2023; Passel and Cohn 2019). About 925,000, or approximately 40 percent of the undocumented immigrant population, live in the metropolitan Los Angeles area, which includes the County of Los Angeles, Orange County, Riverside County, and the County of San Bernardino (Perez et al. 2023; Passel and Cohn 2019). Georgia, on the other hand, is a new immigrant destination, with current estimates suggesting that about 339,000 of the 10.7 million state residents are unauthorized immigrants, primarily from Mexico (Migration Policy Institute 2019). The metropolitan Atlanta area includes Fulton, Gwinnett, DeKalb, Cobb, and Clayton counties and is home to about 197,000 unauthorized immigrants across these five counties (Migration Policy Institute 2019). While the characterization of metropolitan Los Angeles as a traditional immigrant gateway and metropolitan Atlanta as a new immigrant destination is useful for understanding recent trends in undocumented Latinx immigration to each region, these characterizations obscure the long and often complicated history of Latinx communities in each state. For example, as recently as the 1990s, unauthorized immigration to California was a politically divisive issue in the state (HoSang 2010; Hayes-Bautista 2017). In addition, because of its agricultural landscape, Latinx migration to the U.S. South, and specifically to Georgia, has been happening since as far back as 1910 (Weise 2015). These complex regional racial formations, or smaller-scale racial orders (Cheng 2013), are also situated within the broader historical legacies of California, as a former territory of Mexico, and Georgia, as a slave-holding state.

The Latinx History of Metropolitan Los Angeles

California emerged as an immigrant gateway after the World War II era when the Los Angeles metropolitan area became a hub for immigration (Singer 2004). Prior to World War II, however, California had a long and complicated history with Latinxs, and with Mexicans, in particular. California was annexed from Mexico in 1848 under the Treaty of Guadalupe Hidalgo, ushering in a period of confusion about the social, cultural, and economic place of Mexicans in the state (Acuna 1996; Gutierrez 1995). As journalist Juan Gonzalez noted, California was the richest prize of the war with Mexico as gold was discovered shortly after its annexation, creating an influx of Anglo settlers that quickly outnumbered the Mexican and Indigenous populations in the state (Gonzalez 2004). This shift in population dynamics introduced a long and complicated legacy that is relevant for understanding how the proximity of California and Mexico, both geographically and politically, has shaped race relations in the state and the experiences of contemporary Latinx undocumented immigrants.

Latinxs have been a constant presence in California, and continued immigration flows have continued to replenish this population (Jimenez 2008). Starting as early as the 1920s, Mexican migrants became a core part of the agricultural, packing, and canning labor forces in the Los Angeles region (Valadez Torres 2005). In addition to working in these industries, Mexican migrants were also a key part of construction-related industries and the domestic workforce (Valadez Torres 2005). However, with the crash of 1929 and the depression that followed, Mexican migrants, specifically in the Los Angeles area, were a target for deportation. Under the guise of "repatriation," nearly 100,000 Mexican migrants were forced to return to Mexico between 1929 and 1939. By the 1950s, however, and largely due to the Bracero Program, Mexican migration, both documented and undocumented, had grown, and an economic boom in California increased the demand for Mexican labor (Durand et al. 2000). California remained a destination for undocumented Latinx migration through the 1980s. In fact, following the passage of IRCA in 1986, estimates suggest that about 55 percent of undocumented immigrants legalized through the program lived in California; of these, nearly 40 percent lived in Southern California (Durand et al. 2000). During the 1990s, a severe economic recession plagued California, and anti-undocumented-immigrant sentiment rose, culminating in the passage of a series of racialized propositions, including Proposition 209 (banning affirmative action in schools and workplaces), Proposition 227 (eliminating bilingual education), and Proposition 187 (seeking to deny access to public services to undocumented immigrants). Each of these propositions reflected a growing anxiety in the state about the "browning" of California (Ochoa 2004), and the perception of an influx of Latinx undocumented immigrants to the state and the perceived threat they posed (HoSang 2010; Durand et al. 2000; Chavez 2008). As anthropologist Leo Chavez aptly notes, the 1990s saw a proliferation of books, many written by academics, building on the public's fears about a changing nation due to Latinx immigration. The Southern California region was the focus of much of this anxiety around citizenship and national identity (Chavez 2008). This anxiety was on full display during the campaign to pass Proposition 187, also known as the Save Our State initiative, on the 1994 ballot. Proposition 187 proposed to prevent undocumented immigrants from accessing a variety of social services, including healthcare and education, both K–12 and college, and it was the earliest iteration of racialized anti-immigrant policy (Varsanyi 2010).

The group behind Proposition 187 had deep ties to Orange County, California, a county long associated with conservative politics (McGirr 2001). While Orange County has been depicted in popular culture as a predominantly white affluent region, it is a racially, ethnically, and socioeconomically diverse county comprising individual cities that each have their own identities and sociopolitical contexts. Santa Ana, the county seat, is a majority Latinx community, with approximately 75 percent of the population identifying as Hispanic. Westminster, also located in Orange County, is home to the largest Vietnamese American community in the United States. Despite the contemporary racial and ethnic diversity of the region, Orange County has long been a conservative stronghold anchored by communities like Costa Mesa, Huntington Beach, and Yorba Linda. While organizers of the Proposition 187 campaign argued that the campaign was about fiscal responsibility and the rule of law, the racialized and nativist undertones of the campaign could not be ignored (HoSang 2010). The proposition was on the ballot the same year as the 1994 gubernatorial election. Incumbent Republican Governor Pete Wilson was running for a second term, and his campaign embraced the restrictionist message of Proposition 187. In a now infamous campaign commercial, grainy video showed immigrants at the San Diego border crossing the 5 Freeway as a voice booms over the images, "They keep coming." The focus on the U.S.-Mexico border as the site for much of the campaign rhetoric made it clear that Latinx immigrants, and Mexican immigrants more specifically, were the primary threat (Chavez 2008). The message of both Proposition 187 and Pete Wilson's campaign catalyzed the Latinx community, especially in Southern California, where Latinx youth marched out of their schools to protest the proposition. A formal coalition comprising proimmigrant organizations across the state, Californians United Against 187, also challenged the proposition (HoSang 2010). Although there was community mobilization against it, the proposition passed by a two-to-one margin among California voters (HoSang 2010; Schrag 2010). A group of civil rights organizations was prepared with legal challenges, and the U.S. District Court blocked implementation of the law (HoSang 2010; Varsanyi 2010), arguing that it violated the plenary power of the federal government over immigration enforcement. Nevertheless, the furor surrounding the proposition had lasting effects on California's Latinx undocumented immigrant community. During the 1990s and through the 2000s, difficult economic circumstances in California, including a depressed labor market, stricter controls at the San Diego border, and an increasingly hostile anti-immigrant climate, resulted in a rapid shift of Mexican immigrants away from California to new immigrant destinations like Georgia (Durand et al. 2000).

In addition, because of the racialized propositions on the ballot in the late 1990s, including Proposition 187, which heightened anti-immigrant sentiment and public discourse, Latinx undocumented young adults who came of age in the 1990s in California had very similar experiences to Latinx undocumented young adults who came of age in the 2000s in Georgia. Despite this relatively hostile history, California is currently considered a welcoming place for undocumented immigrants. By the 2000s, California and the metropolitan Los Angeles region were firmly established as Latinx-centric locales. The Los Angeles metropolitan area specifically has been at the forefront of integrationist initiatives, including being among the first cities to offer identification in the form of a city ID to unauthorized immigrants. When Arizona passed Senate Bill (SB) 1070, its infamous anti-immigrant law, the Los Angeles City Council voted to cut off business ties with the state. This has and continues to have important material and symbolic implications for unauthorized Latinx immigrants in California, as citizen Latinx co-ethnics are a social, economic, and political presence in the state. While the Latinx community in Atlanta, Georgia, is growing demographically, the same is not true for Latinx unauthorized immigrants living in Georgia, as I discuss in the next section.

The Latinx History of Metropolitan Atlanta

Georgia emerged as a "new immigrant destination" during the 1990s and 2000s, when the overall immigrant population in the metropolitan area grew from less than 10 percent to more than 25 percent in just twenty years (Singer 2004). The influx of Latinx immigrants during this period resulted from several factors, including the passage of IRCA, which led to strain on the labor market in traditional immigrant gateways like Los Angeles (Odem and Lacy 2009; Zuniga and Hernandez-Leon 2009). In addition, during the 1990s, labor economies in the South, including manufacturing, poultry processing, and the service sector, provided new and abundant opportunities for unauthorized immigrants (Lippard and Gallagher 2011; Weeks and Weeks 2010; Odem and Lacy 2009). Economic booms in two distinct Southeast regions—Charlotte, North Carolina, and Atlanta, Georgia—led to an influx of immigrants (Lippard and Gallagher 2011; Weeks and Weeks 2010). The 1996 Olympic Games brought thousands of Mexican construction workers to the Atlanta area, and this migration continued for over two decades (Odem and Lacy 2009). Although between 2009 and 2014 the unauthorized population in Georgia decreased, the state currently has the seventh-largest undocumented immigrant population in the country (Passel and Cohn 2014). Current estimates suggest that about 400,000 of the 10 million state residents are unauthorized immigrants, primarily from Mexico and Guatemala (Passel and Cohn 2014).

While this relatively recent influx of Latinx unauthorized migrants has garnered attention and hostility in the state, historian Julie Weise (2015) argues that the public and scholarly characterization of Georgia as a *new* immigrant destination is inaccurate. Instead, she shows that Mexican migration to the state, although not to Atlanta, began in the late 1950s with a group of about 1,300 braceros who picked cotton alongside African Americans in the southern part of the state. From the 1960s through the 1980s, Georgia's Vidalia sweet onions and peaches brought Mexican migrant farmworkers to the state, and some were able to settle and make a living working other fruit and vegetable crops in the region (Weise 2015). Many of these agricultural workers adjusted their status under the special agricultural worker provisions of IRCA. Yet, overwhelmed labor markets in California and Texas led to a continuous flow of unauthorized migrants to southern Georgia. By 1989, the agricultural labor market in the state had almost completely turned over to Latinx immigrant labor (Weise 2015).

In the northern part of Georgia, predominantly white industrial towns, including Gainesville, Cedartown, and Dalton, recruited Mexican workers to work in carpet mills, although their treatment was considerably more hostile than in southern Georgia. One exception to this harsh treatment was the city of Dalton, where carpet mill owners were able to calm anti-immigrant sentiment and encourage integration initiatives (Weise 2015; Zuniga and Hernandez-Leon 2009). The experiences of Latinx immigrants in the southern and northern parts of the state highlight the complexity of Latinx migration not only to Georgia but also to the new "*viejo*" South (Weise 2015). While both the southern and northern parts of Georgia have had a longer history of Latinx immigration, Latinx undocumented immigration to the Atlanta area began in earnest in the early 1990s in advance of the 1996 Olympic Games.

The migration patterns of immigrants to the Atlanta area followed earlier Mexican migration patterns, including migration first by single, working-class males—some from traditional immigrant destinations such as Los Angeles—followed during the 1990s by increasing numbers of female migrants and children (Odem and Lacy 2009). Interviews with Latinx undocumented young adults in the Atlanta area confirmed this, as many of the participants' fathers continue to work in the construction industry, the industry that first brought them and their families to the region. As with other new immigrant destinations, a polarizing debate has emerged in the South—even as studies showed that, in the late 1990s and early 2000s, some Southerners viewed immigrants as breathing new life into dying towns (Jones 2012; Marrow 2011; Odem and Lacy 2009). Immigrants, even if unauthorized, brought not only economic labor but also commerce to struggling main streets across the South. On the other hand, these studies also suggest that others viewed them as simply "illegals" who take jobs and burden taxpayers (Odem and Lacy 2009), a sentiment that has persisted even as Latinx undocumented immigrants continue to remain in the state and make their homes and lives in these regions.

Odem and Lacy (2009) find that, prior to 2000, before a significant influx of unauthorized immigrants to the Atlanta area, attitudes toward immigrants were either neutral or generally positive. Marrow (2011) comes to a similar conclusion in her in-depth study of immigration to rural North Carolina. However, the turn of the twenty-first century brought deteriorating economic conditions and rapid growth in the Latinx immigrant population, spurring public discourse that emphasized the social and economic costs of immigration (Odem and Lacy 2009). Georgia was one of the first and most aggressive states in the South to seek to limit the rights of unauthorized immigrants to transportation, housing, healthcare, and higher education. Research about the transformation of the South has captured the demographic shifts in the immigrant population. Yet, studies about the incorporation of this group, especially Latinx undocumented young adults, are relatively sparse. In a telling conclusion, Marrow (2011) suggests that while native-born populations seem to be open to immigrant populations, legal status or rather "illegal" status significantly alters the experiences of unauthorized immigrants.

Despite a hostile context, previous research demonstrates that Latinx unauthorized migrants are making their lives in the "New South." They are (re)claiming spaces in the form of churches, storefronts, and neighborhoods. This has proven integral for reproducing a social life and creating integration opportunities for immigrants, undocumented and documented alike (Odem and Lacy 2009; Zuniga and Hernandez-Leon 2009). The remnants of this demographic shift were visible when I was in Atlanta conducting fieldwork. Driving along highways in the Atlanta area, I was attuned to spatial evidence of the presence of Latinxs and other immigrant groups. The Buford Highway, a thirty-mile stretch in the Atlanta area, is the physical and symbolic home of many of these communities, starting in Midtown Atlanta and running through four diverse suburbs of the area, including Brookhaven, Chamblee, Doraville, and Norcross. Along a ten-mile stretch of the highway, you will find various immigrant-owned businesses, including restaurants and grocery stores. The billboard in figure 2, for example, caught my eye as I was driving back from an interview in Norcross, a heavily populated Latinx immigrant community in the Atlanta area.

The juxtaposition of the billboard being in Spanish with the cartoonish and stereotypical image of a "Mexican" signaled to me the ongoing and precarious position of Latinxs in the area and the state. During fieldwork, I learned that the space, both physically and symbolically, that Latinx

FIGURE 2 Norcross, Georgia.

undocumented immigrants have claimed in the area was the result of concerted community-based advocacy efforts and that this has been an ongoing struggle. This parallels previous research that shows that, in the Atlanta area, physical spaces such as streets, parks, and other public locales have become places of conflict (Odem and Lacy 2009). This, coupled with workplace raids, raids at apartment complexes, and regular patrols of immigrant neighborhoods, has stifled the social integration of undocumented immigrants in the Atlanta area.

In late 2014, then-Mayor Kasim Reed established the Mayor's Office of Immigrant Affairs, declaring Atlanta a "welcoming city," an important step forward signaling the city's intention to support and welcome "new arrivals." The Welcoming Atlanta Initiative is currently housed in the Mayor's Office of Immigrant and International Affairs. The continuity of the office has been important for local immigrant communities in Atlanta. Nevertheless, Latinx undocumented immigrants living in Atlanta and the surrounding area continue to face significant legal barriers and challenges. For example, when President Obama announced the Deferred Action for Parental Arrivals (DAPA) and DACA+ programs, proposed programs that would have offered similar protections to the DACA program, two different state legislators proposed bills that would bar DAPA recipients from being eligible for driver's licenses. In the wake of the announcement of the DAPA and DACA+ programs, similar bills were proposed seeking to revoke DACA recipients' driver's licenses. In

February 2016, state senator Josh McKoon also proposed that the term "illegal alien" be added next to driver's licenses issued to undocumented immigrants in the state (Foley 2016). Georgia was also one of twenty-six states that joined the legal challenge to DAPA and DACA+, asserting that implementation of these programs would create a significant burden to the state. When Donald Trump was elected president in 2016, the Atlanta area became a key site for immigration enforcement. With a series of punitive policies and an ongoing onslaught of proposed legislation seeking to limit the rights of undocumented immigrants and DACA recipients in the state, the everyday lives of Latinx undocumented immigrants in Georgia continue to be difficult. In the next two sections, I examine how the interactions between federal and state laws and policies shape the lived experiences of Latinx undocumented immigrants in both Los Angeles, California, and Atlanta, Georgia.

The Legacy of *Plyler v. Doe*: The Federal Immigration Landscape

In 1982, the Supreme Court of the United States held in *Plyler v. Doe*[1] that undocumented immigrant children had a right to a public education through high school graduation. The case challenged the State of Texas's implementation of a fee charged only to undocumented immigrant children, effectively excluding them from public education (Motomura 2014). Justice Powell, who wrote the Court's opinion, argued that denying undocumented immigrant children access to public education would create a "lifetime hardship on a discrete class of children not accountable for their disabling status" (*Plyler v. Doe* as cited in Pabon Lopez 2005, 17). The opinion reflected a tacit acknowledgment of the importance of education for creating a pathway to upward social mobility, or in the case of undocumented children, at least avoiding a state-sanctioned downward trajectory. The *Plyler* precedent has endured for over thirty years (Motomura 2014; Olivas 2011). While *Plyler* is generally considered a historic legal victory for Latinxs, one of *Plyler*'s unintended legacies has been to open the door to an uncertain future as undocumented young people leave the K–12 system (Gonzales et al. 2015; Olivas 2011).

---

1. *Plyler v. Doe*, 457 U.S. 202 (1982).

To ameliorate some of this uncertainty, undocumented youth have tirelessly advocated for over ten years for the passage of the Development Relief and Education for Alien Minors (DREAM) Act. Initially introduced in 2001, the DREAM Act would have provided a pathway to citizenship for undocumented immigrant youth who meet certain requirements. Initially the DREAM Act was focused on educational attainment and community service. It has been introduced four times, in 2007, 2009, 2010, and again in 2011, and over time has received bipartisan support—although some speculate that this came at a cost. With each introduction, the language of the DREAM Act became more restrictive and focused primarily on rewarding "deserving" undocumented young people. By 2010, the language included military service and a "high moral character" standard. Yet with each iteration, the undocumented youth movement also grew in strength and influence. By 2010, passing the DREAM Act eclipsed comprehensive immigration reform as the central fight of the national immigrant rights movement, despite considerable tension between passing the DREAM Act and pushing for comprehensive immigration reform (Nicholls 2013). While it came closest to passing in 2010, the DREAM Act has never passed, signaling a larger societal ambivalence about providing a pathway to citizenship to undocumented immigrants, even the most "palatable"—English-speaking, high-achieving, "innocent" children.

A short two years after the DREAM Act's failure in 2010, President Barack Obama announced the DACA program in the Rose Garden on the White House lawn, and in sharing his rationale for using his presidential power to provide immigration relief, he remarked:

> These are young people who study in our schools, they play in our neighborhoods, they're friends with our kids, they pledge allegiance to our flag. They are Americans in their heart, in their minds, in every single way but one: on paper . . . Put yourself in their shoes. Imagine you've done everything right your entire life—studied hard, worked hard, maybe even graduated at the top of your class—only to suddenly face the threat of deportation to a country that you know nothing about, with a language that you may not even speak. . . . Effective immediately, the Department of Homeland Security is taking steps to lift the shadow of deportation from these young people. . . . Now, let's be clear—this is not amnesty, this

is not immunity. This is not a path to citizenship. It's not a permanent fix. This is a temporary stopgap measure that lets us focus our resources wisely while giving a degree of relief and hope to talented, driven, patriotic young people.

President Obama's announcement echoed the discourse that was strategically employed by the undocumented student movement to advocate for the passage of the DREAM Act. DACA ushered in a key legal shift for undocumented immigrant youth because it granted a two-year temporary stay of deportation for eligible undocumented young adults who came to the United States before the age of sixteen.[2] Symbolically, DACA represented the first major federal commitment since IRCA that acknowledges, albeit with temporary relief, the continued presence of undocumented immigrants in the United States. In addition to deportation relief, DACA recipients do not continue to accrue a period of unlawful presence, and they are eligible to apply for work authorization. In addition, DACA has opened the door to other key benefits for undocumented young adults, including driver's licenses. Since its introduction, nearly 800,000 undocumented young people have received DACA.

Research examining the impact of DACA on recipients has been generally positive. Two years after the program's implementation, 89 percent of DACA recipients reported getting a driver's license, significantly reducing the risk of driving-related infractions (Wong et al. 2015). In addition, 69 percent reported getting a job with better pay, and 92 percent of those enrolled in school pursued educational opportunities that they would not have pursued otherwise (Wong et al. 2015). As DACA approached the ten-year mark, these numbers held steady, with 59 percent of DACA recipients reporting that they got a job with better pay, 81 percent reporting that they were able to earn more money and become

---

2. Other requirements include: (1) continuous presence in the United States from 2007, (2) under the age of thirty-one as of June 15, 2012, (3) physical presence in the United States on June 15, 2012, (4) entrance into the United States without inspection before June 15, 2012, (5) current enrollment in school, a high school diploma, GED, or honorable discharge from armed forces or Coast Guard, and (6) no felony or serious misdemeanor convictions and (a person who) does not pose a serious threat to national security.

financially independent, and 78 percent reporting they were able to earn more money to support their family financially (Wong et al. 2024). While these results are positive, they obscure key issues that I explore in this book; for example, much of this success varies by state. As President Obama noted in his announcement, DACA is a temporary relief program with no pathway to citizenship. Underscoring the political vulnerability of DACA was the President's announcement in November 2014 of the Deferred Action for Parents of Americans and Lawful Permanent Residents (DAPA) program and the expansion of DACA to a broader group of individuals, referred to as DACA+. Both programs were under a temporary injunction restricting implementation. The Supreme Court heard the case in April 2016, and a ruling in June 2016 left both programs in limbo as an evenly divided four–four court let the injunction stand, essentially blocking either program from ever taking effect. In 2017, the Trump administration revoked the order, ending the program. A few of the undocumented youths I interviewed expressed apprehension about the legal challenges to DAPA and DACA+ and wondered if DACA would also be threatened. In addition, undocumented young adults in both California and Georgia expressed concern about the 2016 presidential election. In the run up to the Republican presidential primary in 2016, several nominees not only threatened DACA but also proposed mass deportations, and further fortification of the U.S.-Mexico border. Given this rhetoric, Latinx undocumented young adults expressed uncertainty about the continued viability of DACA, and their fears were affirmed when, in September 2017, then-President Donald Trump announced the end of the DACA program. The case made its way to the Supreme Court. The Supreme Court held in June 2020 that the program's termination was not legal, preserving DACA for current beneficiaries. Nevertheless, a new generation of undocumented young people are not able to apply for DACA, finding themselves in a continued state of limbo, and increasing the importance of place in their lives.

State Legal Contexts: Comparing California and Georgia

While immigration law and policy fall under the purview of the federal government, immigrants ultimately settle in states and localities. How undocumented immigrants are welcomed (or not) in these states and localities has a profound impact on their day-to-day lives (Marrow 2011). The absence of comprehensive immigration reform, coupled with the movement of undocumented immigrant populations away from traditional gateways, has created varying contexts of reception within the United States. As a result, states and localities have responded differently to the influx of undocumented immigrants, with most states responding by restricting rights and benefits. A prime example of this is Arizona's SB 1070, which was signed by Governor Jan Brewer in 2010. Following Arizona, several other states, including Georgia, passed similarly restrictive bills. To gauge a state's relative openness and hostility, I examine a few types of laws that impact undocumented immigrants. These include (1) an omnibus punitive immigration law, (2) laws mandating an employment verification system (E-Verify), (3) laws requiring applicants for public benefits to prove their citizenship or immigration status, (4) laws addressing immigrant access to higher education, (5) laws granting driver's licenses, and (6) laws granting professional licenses, for example, to be a lawyer or a hairstylist. In each of these areas of law, California and Georgia have taken very different stances.

Although California does not have a restrictive statewide immigration law, as I detailed earlier in this chapter, California voters passed Proposition 187 in 1994, one of the first anti-immigrant omnibus laws in the nation. In 2011, Georgia passed House Bill (HB) 87, also known as the Illegal Immigration Reform and Control Act, which included provisions that made it a misdemeanor to be an undocumented immigrant, imposed penalties on any individual assisting an undocumented immigrant, and required local law enforcement officers to determine an individual's immigration status. Also included in HB 87 were provisions requiring that employers use E-Verify, in contrast to California, where E-Verify is voluntary for employers. While conducting fieldwork in Georgia, I learned that this shift significantly impacted the day-to-day lives of undocumented Latinx young adults, including significantly increasing fear and anxiety for themselves and their families. In Georgia, the shift in state context started in the late 1990s with the rise in migration to the state. In 1996, Georgia passed legislation making English the official language of the state, part of a broader English-only movement that led to twenty states passing official English-language laws. In response to claims that translation was costly, particularly for local and state governments, SB 519 stated that all official government documents and meetings should be in English. There is no statewide law in California declaring English the state's official language. However, in 1998, California voters passed Proposition 227, also known as English for the Children. The law significantly changed bilingual education in the state, requiring students to be taught primarily in English and parents to opt into bilingual education after one year. It was not repealed until 2016. Other laws that impact undocumented immigrants include those addressing access to driver's licenses, which in Georgia are only available to DACA recipients and in California are available to any undocumented immigrant. Various professionals require state licensing, including teachers, hair stylists, lawyers, estheticians, and doctors. In California, undocumented immigrants can pursue these career pathways and apply for a license as guaranteed through SB 1159, enacted in 2015. In Georgia, undocumented immigrants cannot apply for state professional licenses.

For the undocumented 1.5 generation, the current legal landscape is problematic precisely because of the unintended consequences of contradictory federal and state immigration laws and policies that leave many undocumented young adults in a state of limbo, especially as they transition out of high school (Gonzales 2016). In twenty-five states, including California, undocumented immigrant students who meet certain requirements can attend college and pay in-state resident tuition (ISRT), and sixteen of these states offer or will offer state financial aid to students who meet certain criteria, regardless of their immigration status (National Immigration Law Center 2024). Just four states, including California, also offer state and institutional financial aid to undocumented students. Access to state and institutional aid considerably eases the financial burden of paying for college, especially given the rising costs of receiving a college degree. On the other end of the spectrum, three states, including Georgia, require undocumented students to pay out-of-state tuition at public colleges. Out-of-state tuition can range from two to four times the in-state tuition rate.

In 2011, the Georgia Board of Regents, the governing body of the University System of Georgia, restricted undocumented immigrants from attending the most competitive colleges in the state under Policy 4.1.6, which stated that "a person who is not lawfully present in the United States shall not be eligible for admission to any University System institution, which, for the two most recent academic years, did not admit all academically qualified applicants."[3] Since 2011, the policy has consistently applied to the state's flagship public institution, the University of Georgia, located in Athens, as well as Georgia State University and the Georgia Institute of Technology, both located in Atlanta. During interviews, I learned that these three universities were often the top college choices of undocumented students in the state. Yet, they could not attend. In addition, undocumented immigrants must pay out-of-state tuition at *any* public college or university, including less prestigious state campuses and two-year colleges and universities. During interviews, respondents from Georgia shared that the average cost of attending college, even a two-year college, was three times the amount an in-state resident would pay. Thus, it was Policy 4.3.4 that created the greatest barrier to college attendance.

Restrictive policies, like those in Georgia, are a relatively new phenomenon, with most of these laws and policies emerging after 2010. Previous research about the impact of in-state residency tuition policies on college enrollment is mixed. Some studies find that ISRT policies increase college enrollment among Latinx undocumented immigrants (Kaushal 2008; Flores 2010). More recent research suggests that ISRT policies do not increase college enrollment but that restrictive policies like those in Georgia have a negative impact (Bozick et al. 2016). These studies highlight an empirical quandary—What are the consequences of welcoming or restrictive higher education policies for the educational access and experiences of Latinx undocumented young adults? In chapter 3, I specifically examine the ramifications of these higher educational policies for Latinx undocumented young adults in California and Georgia. While higher education policies have the most direct impact on the lives of Latinx undocumented young adults, *especially* for the participants in this study, the lives of undocumented immigrants are shaped by a patchwork of laws that influence their day-to-day lives.

Table 1 summarizes the different policy landscapes of each state in areas that impact undocumented immigrants, including undocumented immigrant young people.

---

3. When I started this study, undocumented immigrants were restricted from attending the top five public colleges in the states; that shifted over time to only apply to the top three colleges in the state.

TABLE 1 Comparison of state laws and policies aimed at unauthorized immigrants

Law or policy	California	Georgia
Restrictive statewide immigration law	No statewide policy **Prop 187**: Passed in 1994	**HB 87**: Enacted in 2011 Law enforcement officers can check the immigration status of any individual who cannot produce identification Blocked by Supreme Court: Provision making it a felony to "transport, harbor, or conceal an illegal immigrant"
E-Verify:	**AB 1236**: Enacted in 2012 Optional E-Verify: State and localities prohibited from mandating E-Verify; can be used voluntarily	**HB 87**: Enacted in 2011 Strict E-Verify: All employers must check employee's eligibility against the Social Security and Department of Homeland Security database
English-only or official English-language law	No statewide policy **Prop 227**: Passed in 1998	**SB 519**: Enacted in 1996 Requires government documents and meetings in English
State IDs and driver's licenses	**AB 60**: Signed in 2013 Driver's licenses for undocumented immigrants	Driver's licenses only for DACA recipients

Professional licenses	**SB 1159**: Enacted in 2015. Individuals do not have to disclose either citizenship status or immigration status for purposes of licensure	Does not offer professional licenses
Higher education access	Undocumented immigrants can attend any college or university in the state	**BOR Policy 4.1.6**: Undocumented immigrants barred from attending the three most prestigious public colleges and universities
Higher education: In-state residency tuition	**AB 540**: Enacted in 2001. Eligible undocumented immigrants can pay in-state residency tuition	**BOR Policy 4.3.4**: Prohibits undocumented immigrants from paying in-state tuition
Higher education: State financial aid	**AB 130** and **AB 131**: Enacted in 2011. AB 130: Undocumented immigrants eligible for private financial aid. AB 131: Undocumented immigrants eligible for state financial aid	No statewide policy

Sources: The National Immigration Law Center; The National Conference for State Legislatures.

Note: AB, Assembly Bill; BOR, Board of Regents; DACA, Deferred Action for Childhood Arrivals; HB, House Bill.

Conclusion

In 2012, the U.S. Supreme Court struck down some of the harshest provisions of restrictive omnibus laws, such as SB 1070 and HB 87 in *Arizona v. United States*[4]. These state-level laws, coupled with federal inaction on comprehensive immigration reform, have created a hostile context of reception for unauthorized immigrants, both locally and more broadly at the national level (Portes and Rumbaut 2001; Portes et al. 2005). Restrictive anti-immigrant omnibus policies have had the intended effect of increased scrutiny of the undocumented immigrant community. In contrast, since the 2000s, states like California have enacted laws that integrate undocumented immigrants, including access to driver's licenses and professional state licenses. The result is a fractured landscape for undocumented immigrants. Yet, states like California have also chosen a path of inclusion. While the proliferation of restrictive policies in various states, including those in the New South, has slowed considerably, anti-immigrant rhetoric and sentiment are at an all-time high. Where undocumented immigrants, including undocumented Latinx young people, grow up and live is becoming increasingly important for their transition to and through adulthood.

In this chapter, I offered an in-depth look at the laws and policies that impacted the daily lives of Latinx undocumented young people and their families in California and Georgia—their legal ecologies. Latinx undocumented young people's experiences of the law were also shaped by the racial dynamics of their localities, including the histories of Latinx immigration to their respective regions. While there is strong evidence for the characterization of California as a welcoming locale and Georgia as hostile, this can obscure the complexity of the experiences of Latinx undocumented young people and their search for belonging. In the following chapters, I unpack this complexity and examine the consequences of shifting, sometimes contradictory, political and legal landscapes for Latinx undocumented young adults. I explore the material implications of this for their educational pathways and futures. I also examine how their varied legal ecologies shape their ideas about race, ethnicity, citizenship, and activism.

---

4. *Arizona v. United States*, 567 U.S. 87 (2012).

CHAPTER 2

GROWING UP UNDOCUMENTED IN SHIFTING LEGAL CONTEXTS

While the sociopolitical context in California is generally characterized as welcoming to immigrants in contrast to Georgia, which is characterized as hostile, differences between the two places are much more nuanced than this binary suggests. In chapter 1, I discussed how historical, racial, and legal dynamics shaped the contexts in which undocumented young adults lived. In the remainder of the book, I trace the lived reality of undocumented young adults in these two locales, showing how, from postmigration childhood through young adulthood, participants were developing a complex understanding of the implications of intersecting federal, state, and local political contexts for their daily lives and futures, or the *legal ecologies* of undocumented young adults. An important layer in the lives, and therefore the legal ecologies, of undocumented young adults are their families, specifically their parents, who are often themselves undocumented. A growing body of research shows the collateral consequences of the U.S. immigration policy for families, especially for those in mixed-status households, with a focus on U.S.-born children of undocumented parents (Enriquez 2015). While the young people in this study were themselves undocumented, in childhood, their own legal status was not as salient to how they navigated the world. Much like U.S.-born children of undocumented parents, their day-to-day lives were primarily influenced by their parents' undocumented status. Sociologists have identified the intergenerational impacts of immigration laws and refer to these impacts as multigenerational punishment (Enriquez 2015), shared vulnerability (Abrego 2019), and collective negotiation of illegality (Rodriguez Vega 2018). These concepts capture key nuances of the experiences of children of undocumented parents and share an understanding of the collateral consequences of punitive and exclusionary immigration laws for families, regardless of an individual family member's legal status.

Punitive immigration policies have both material and symbolic consequences. As sociologist Laura Enriquez (2015) finds, exclusionary immigration policies govern four dimensions of mixed-status families' lives, including fear of deportation, driving, travel, and employment. In each of these areas, navigating everyday life is made harder by intersecting immigration policies at the state and federal levels. These impacts are material precisely because they have a tangible effect on the lives of children with undocumented parents. As previous studies show, living in a household with undocumented parents increases the structural barriers children face—making them more likely to live in poverty and have related experiences like food insecurity (Suárez-Orozco et al. 2011; Yoshikawa 2011). Distinct from their U.S.-born peers, for undocumented young people more specifically, pathways to social mobility are also blocked as undocumented immigrants are barred from accessing key social services and educational and employment opportunities (Abrego 2019).

Beyond the material impacts of exclusionary immigration policies, children of undocumented parents are attuned to the fears and anxieties their parents feel and demonstrate a profound understanding of the threat posed by punitive immigration policies and a hostile sociopolitical context (Rodriguez Vega 2018). These impacts are symbolic because they signal a clear boundary between "us" and "them." In the case of children who themselves may be undocumented or in mixed-status families, anti-immigrant rhetoric that paints undocumented immigrants as lawbreakers and/or threats sends an important message about who is included and who should be excluded. Drawing from art-based work with children in Arizona, Silvia Rodriguez Vega reveals how children make sense of punitive policies and anti-immigrant discourse in places like California and Arizona. The children Rodriguez Vega worked with conveyed not only fears and anxieties related to the detention and deportation of their parents but also an understanding of the underlying logic that explained why their families were vulnerable, including racist and nativist beliefs about Latinxs, and Mexicans, more specifically. While not surprising, it is important to be reminded that children and adolescents are incredibly perceptive and aware of the dynamics in their sociopolitical environments.

Notions of multigenerational punishment, shared vulnerability, and shared negotiation of illegality provide key insights into the experiences of the Latinx undocumented young adults I got to know. Although they themselves were undocumented, they would come to know the full impact of their status as they transitioned out of high school and into adulthood. As children and adolescents, they were developing an understanding of what it meant to be undocumented in their respective locales. In the Los Angeles area, some interviewees described a hostile climate before and during the campaign to pass Proposition 187, one of the first anti-immigrant laws in the country. This was like the context Latinx undocumented young adults in the Atlanta area described emerging in the early 2000s. In fact, the hostility undocumented immigrants experienced in California in the 1990s led to a migration of undocumented immigrants out of the state to places like Georgia. But young people in Los Angeles and Orange County also described a noticeable positive shift in the sociopolitical context after the passage and subsequent repeal of Proposition 187, the result of increased mobilization by immigrant and nonimmigrant Latinxs in the state. Young people in Atlanta also described a noticeable shift during the 1990s through the 2000s, from a more laissez-faire approach to an increasingly hostile climate toward undocumented immigrants. In both locales, undocumented young people described an awareness of shared vulnerability. That vulnerability would become more acute as they themselves transitioned into high school and began to interact more directly with structures and institutions that were either inclusionary or exclusionary based on where they lived.

Despite the fears and anxieties undocumented young people shared about their parents' immigration status when they were growing up, they also described childhoods that were filled with a sense of security within the context of their families. While their childhoods were punctured by magnified moments (Rodriguez 2018; Hochschild 1994) in the form of instances of discrimination or acute moments of anxiety that stayed with them, they also shared that their parents did their best to make them feel safe. In fact, later in young adulthood, as these young people developed a better sense of how their own undocumented status would influence their lives, they described drawing inspiration and motivation from their parents' experiences as undocumented people in the United States. While young people generally did not identify specific laws and policies in direct terms when recounting their childhood experiences, they did describe their perceptions of key shifts in the political climates in both California and Georgia. In California, for example, following the passage of Proposition 187, the young people shared how policy changes in the state (e.g., AB 540, the driver's license laws) signaled a radical change in the state's orientation toward undocumented immigrants. In contrast, in Georgia, there was a sense of heightening attention toward undocumented immigrants, especially following September 11, 2001. The shifts in state-level immigration policies signaled a move away from what undocumented young adults described as a laissez-faire orientation toward undocumented immigrants to an increasingly exclusionary and hostile orientation.

In the remainder of this chapter, I show how Latinx undocumented young adults' childhood memories reflected the increasing importance of place in shaping the transition to adulthood for this group. Their experiences in childhood were influenced by the local dynamics of the histories of immigration to Los Angeles and Atlanta, as I discussed in chapter 1. These dynamics and histories significantly impacted the young people's day-to-day experiences, reflecting Los Angeles's status as a "traditional immigrant destination" and Atlanta's status as a "new immigrant destination." Los Angeles, a traditional immigrant gateway, provided a buffer for young people and their families, even while the state was coming out of a recent period of high anti-immigrant sentiment in the wake of the passage of Proposition 187, one of the first anti-immigrant laws in the nation. In Atlanta, the perception amongst the non-Latinx population of rapidly shifting demographics spurred anti-immigrant hostility aimed primarily at Latinxs and ushered in policies and practices that were designed to make day-to-day life difficult for undocumented immigrants, like House Bill (HB) 87 and the Board of Regents Policies 4.1.6 and 4.3.4.

In both locales, participants discussed how their parents' undocumented status shaped how they navigated daily family life as children and helped them form early commitments to pursuing a college degree as a way of recognizing their parents' sacrifices during and after migration to the United States. The transition through and out of high school is the focus of the next chapter, where I discuss how changes in college access policies in California and Georgia dramatically shaped the college-going pathways of participants and their understanding of the role their undocumented status would play in their unfolding futures. In this chapter, however, I focus on the period before participants transitioned into high school, as it was in these earlier years of their lives that young people caught glimpses of the vulnerabilities associated with undocumented status. I examine how participants' understanding and experience of their legal status as young adults were shaped by three key factors in their childhood: place, early schooling experiences, and memories of their parents' experiences of discrimination.

Place factored prominently in participants' childhoods as the sociopolitical contexts in both California and Georgia were shifting during the 1990s through the 2010s. These shifting dynamics, coupled with the unique migration histories of the Los Angeles and Atlanta areas, were key factors in shaping participants' recollections of their childhood. Place also shaped their transition into school as the Los Angeles and Orange County regions had long been home to Latinxs, and many of the schools and communities in the area had majority Latinx student populations and employed Latinx teachers. In contrast, the Atlanta area's emerging status as a destination for undocumented immigrants meant that the schools in the area were not as prepared to welcome newly arrived undocumented Latinx students. In both locales, during childhood, young people described an awareness of their parents' vulnerabilities as undocumented immigrants, an awareness that grew as they moved through childhood and into adolescence and as they eventually came to learn of their own legal status and its implications for their futures.

Growing Up Undocumented in Traditional and New Destinations

"It Was Comforting": Context of Reception in Metropolitan Los Angeles

The metropolitan Los Angeles area covers a vast expanse and includes both Los Angeles and Orange Counties. It is the second-largest metropolitan area in the United States in terms of population, just behind New York City. On the ground, or in the car, to be more precise, the metropolitan Los Angeles area starts in Los Angeles proper. As one moves south along the 5 Freeway—the major thoroughfare connecting the Los Angeles-Long Beach-Anaheim metropolitan statistical area—one is taken through densely packed communities rich in their own urban identities and local dynamics, including many of the places undocumented young adults call home. In certain neighborhoods in central Los Angeles and communities surrounding the city, the history and culture of Latinxs are everywhere, from the names of streets to the restaurants and stores that line the streets and the presence of vendors selling chili-spiced fruits and other snacks. The 5 Freeway connects Los Angeles to Santa Ana, a hub of immigrant rights organizing and Latinx culture in Orange County, historically a politically conservative county. Santa Ana itself is four-fifths Latinx and boasts a mayor and city government with strong Latinx representation. One can walk down 4th Street in Santa Ana, *Calle Cuatro*, and hear music in Spanish being played outside stores selling quinceañera dresses. While Santa Ana and other communities in metropolitan Los Angeles and across Orange County are experiencing gentrification, the childhood memories of Latinx undocumented young adults reflect a time when the population in their neighborhoods was predominantly and vibrantly Latinx, which made an important difference in helping them feel a sense of community.

Haciel migrated to a predominantly Latinx neighborhood in central Los Angeles in 2005 at the age of ten. After she, her three-year-old sister, and her six-year-old brother landed in Tijuana from Mexico City, they parted ways with their mother so they could cross the border with another family. Haciel distinctly remembers that, as the oldest, she was told, "Okay, if anything happens, you have to be strong. You have to take care of them. You're responsible because you're the oldest." Through tears, she recalled that she and her brother and sister were caught and held at the border because they were using someone else's papers. Because it was the weekend, they were held in the detention center until their mother could come pick them up on Monday morning. In addition, because of their age difference, Haciel was separated from her younger siblings and was distraught because she could not take care of them as she had promised her mother. After this harrowing experience, Haciel, her siblings, and her mother eventually made their way to the Los Angeles area to reunite with her father, who himself had migrated to the United States when Haciel was just three years old.

During our interview, Haciel explained that the trauma of this early experience was mitigated in part by moving to a predominantly Latinx neighborhood. Although she did not refer to Los Angeles as a "traditional Latinx immigrant gateway," Haciel and respondents who migrated to Los Angeles and the surrounding Southern California area during the 1990s and early 2000s described their transition as less shocking than they anticipated. She reflected on her first impressions of her community, where her family continues to live:

> I would like to say one hundred percent Latino. I mean, when we got there, I was like, "Why is everyone speaking Spanish?" I was surprised because I was like, "Okay." It was comforting to go to a city where at least other people knew the language that I spoke. I didn't feel too out of place.

Haciel's description of her neighborhood as comforting because of the presence of other Latinxs who spoke Spanish echoes the experiences of Latinx undocumented young adults who migrated to the Los Angeles area. Miriam migrated to a predominantly Latinx community located about an hour outside of Los Angeles in San Bernardino County when she was six years old. She described it as "a small boring place. There's predominantly Hispanic people, so I never really felt out of place." Both Miriam and Haciel believed that the fact that other Hispanics were not only physically present but also made up most of the community helped them not to "feel out of place," as they both described. This sense of "not feeling out of place" was the result of both the presence of other Latinxs and the sense that many of their family members, neighbors, and friends may also be undocumented or, as participants shared, *sin papeles*—without papers.

In contrast to the experiences of undocumented young adults in Atlanta, described later in this chapter, respondents in the Los Angeles area described life in communities where they shared not only an ethnic background but also a presumed legal status with others living there. Eduardo, who migrated to a community on the outskirts of the City of Los Angeles, pointed out that "Most of the people there are Hispanic.

There's a lot of undocumented. The undocumented community is big." Alejandra, who migrated when she was eleven years old, stated during our interview:

> I obviously knew I was undocumented the second I crossed the border . . . it was just in my head that I didn't have papers . . . but throughout the whole school years it wasn't a problem; no one really cares. Especially in L.A., because a lot of people are undocumented, so I guess it's common and you don't really talk about it. My school is pre-K–12, and it's like 99 percent Latino. So, I grew up with pure Hispanic people, so there was no questioning about it [her undocumented status].

Rather than creating a stigma in their local communities, the equation of being Latinx and undocumented paradoxically provided respondents with a sense of protection.

Karina immigrated when she was four years old, and while she described her journey as "very easy," she did remember being aware that she, her brother, and her mother were not together during the trip. As Karina shared: "Both me and my brother came as my cousins. I have a cousin who is a year younger than me, and I just passed as I was her. And my brother passed as one of my cousins who is a year older than him." While Karina's brother slept, she remembered being aware and wondering, "Where's my mom? Where's my dad?" To calm Karina, her aunt gave her a dollar, and she shared, "I held that dollar and I remember falling asleep and waking up . . . and the first night, I just remember my dad holding me and saying we're going to talk, let's talk. And we talked the entire night about how we were in Mexico and how he was." Because Karina had vivid memories of her crossing and being reunited with her dad, she grew up knowing she was not born in the United States but was unaware of how her undocumented status would shape her life. After initially living in Los Angeles, Karina and her family eventually moved to Orange County.

As her family settled in Orange County, Karina described a childhood marked by the awareness that she "wasn't from here." While her parents told her and her brother they were not born here, she described a childhood that generally mirrored the experiences of other Latinx undocumented young adults in the Los Angeles and Orange County areas. Many were aware that they were not born here and were not from here. Still, the demographic makeup of their communities, including a shared ethnoracial identity with other Latinxs, mitigated the salience of their undocumented status in childhood. While I am not suggesting that undocumented young adults and their families felt no fear or stigma because of their status, Los Angeles's and Orange County's shared history as a traditional immigrant gateway mitigated some of the hostility that respondents described in Atlanta, Georgia. In addition, the move in the state toward more accommodating laws and policies during the late 1990s and through the 2000s played a significant role in creating the perception of a welcoming political context, a stark contrast to how Latinx undocumented young adults described the political context in Atlanta.

"Life Is Hard Here": Context of Reception in Metropolitan Atlanta

For Latinx undocumented young adults in Atlanta, their experiences of growing up were shaped by both Georgia's status as a "new immigrant destination" *and* the proliferation of restrictive laws in the state. Much of the growth in the Latinx immigrant population began in the mid-1990s as Atlanta was hosting the 1996 Olympics, and a large construction workforce was needed (Wickert 2016). The Olympics was not the only catalyst for Latinx immigrant migration to Georgia. Other construction work and jobs in poultry plants and agriculture all drew Latinxs to the state starting in the mid-1990s through the 2000s. In addition, undocumented Latinx immigrants in other states like California, whose voters had passed Proposition 187 in 1994, were also drawn to the state by the promise of more work and, initially, a more laissez-faire attitude toward immigrants.

Like Los Angeles, Atlanta is a sprawling metropolitan area made up of a vibrant central city surrounded by neighborhoods and communities, each with their own character. From the Hartfield-Jackson Atlanta International Airport southeast of Atlanta, to Decatur, where Emory University is located, Atlanta has been growing since the turn of the twenty-first century. Two of the three universities undocumented students are barred from attending, the Georgia Institute of Technology and Georgia State University, are in the Midtown and Downtown areas. While the public transportation system (the MARTA) is expanding, Atlanta is a car-dependent city. As one navigates the stretch of freeways connecting central Atlanta to its outlying suburbs, one can appreciate the unique character and history of each neighborhood and community. Like Los Angeles, there are pockets of the Atlanta area that house vibrant Latinx communities. Gwinnett County is home to Norcross and Lawrenceville, two of the communities with the largest Latinx populations in the Atlanta area. As you drive along the Buford Highway, a major thoroughfare connecting Atlanta to the city of Buford, one passes an array of restaurants and businesses showcasing the vibrant energy immigrants have brought to the region. About seventy miles outside of Atlanta is the community of Athens, Georgia, home to the University of Georgia, the state's flagship university. Although the university anchors Athens, the surrounding area is rural and has long drawn Latinx immigrants. In the wake of "the ban," Latinx undocumented young adults in Atlanta and Athens became more connected as the University of Georgia became an important site for activism, and Freedom University, an underground nonprofit educational organization founded by a coalition of undocumented students, documented student allies, immigrant rights activists, and professors from the University of Georgia in 2011 (Freedom University website, 2021).

Undocumented young adults who migrated to the metropolitan Atlanta area, especially those who migrated before 2000, before the rapid increase in the Latinx unauthorized population, described being the first family or one of very few Hispanic families in their communities. Luisa, who came to the United States in 1991 at two months old with her mother and her sisters, shared that her parents were the first Hispanic family in their rural community about an hour outside Atlanta, close to Athens. By third grade, in 2001, the demographics of her community were changing, and Luisa and her sisters became translators for others. During our interview, she explained:

> I was mainly translating for her [a recently arrived Hispanic student] because she came at that age, third grade, and so I was working with her on everything. And it was really interesting because my second eldest sister was also doing that; she must have been in seventh or eighth grade. I mean, there was no Hispanic adult to be able to do any translating or interpreting for the kids.

By the time Luisa graduated from high school in 2009, there were at least twenty Hispanic students in her graduating class and many more Hispanic students in the grades below. This shift in the racial demographics of the metropolitan Atlanta area had two distinct but related outcomes that shaped how respondents perceived the political and community context. The increase in the Latinx population during the early 2000s, coupled with a declining economy and fears following the September 11 attacks, increased anti-immigrant sentiment in the state, aimed primarily at undocumented immigrants and the Latinx community (Browne and Odem 2012). On the other hand, as Latinx communities increased in size, Latinx enclaves began to form in various parts of the metropolitan Atlanta area, including in the areas of Chamblee, Doraville, Roswell, and Lawrenceville. While the proliferation of Latinx stores, Spanish-language radio stations and newspapers, and organizations serving Latinxs created a sense of community for Latinx undocumented immigrants, there was also a backlash, which resulted in respondents describing a shift in their daily experiences of hostility.

During our interview, Arturo described how he experienced a shift in the political climate starting around 2008, and he tied this to the recession. During this time, Arturo was leaving middle school and headed into high school, a period of his life that he remembered as difficult. As he moved into high school:

> I do remember being on the, on the bus one day, and it was, it was a white friend of mine, he was like, are you illegal and it's just like that. . . . In high school, freshman year towards the end, that's when it started really hitting me; it affected me really negatively because HB 87 was proposed. Well, I should backtrack. I do remember the raids. They were doing poultry raids under the Bush administration, and so they would come into the factory, and my dad lost his job because of that.

Although Arturo was an adolescent when the political climate shifted, he was aware of the change from what might be considered a more live-and-let-live attitude toward undocumented immigrants to a more noticeably hostile climate. Arturo describes both his own awareness of heightened attention toward undocumented immigrants through the introduction

of HB 87, a punitive state-level immigration law, and the proliferation
and collateral consequences of immigration enforcement raids at workplaces. In 2008, there were several high-profile raids of poultry processing plants, including in Postville, Iowa, and at the Pilgrim's Pride plants
in Texas, Tennessee, and West Virginia (Burgdofer 2008). In 2005, there
were raids at the poultry processing plant in Stillmore, Georgia, a rural town located in southeast Georgia about three hours from Atlanta.
While Arturo did not specify how his dad lost his job, during periods of
heightened workplace enforcement, employers may fire employees who
cannot provide documentation that they have legal permission to work
to guard against workplace raids, a consequence of increased employer
sanctions under the 1986 Immigration Reform and Control Act (IRCA)
(Stuesse 2016). Employers will use Social Security "No Match" letters
to intimidate employees, although this is not the primary purpose of
these letters. They are meant to inform employers that their employees
must verify their documents. However, when an employee receives a
No Match letter, they are faced with a choice: continue working knowing they will not be able to verify their documents or leave their job.
Workplace raids, no matter where they happen, can have lasting impacts.
Workplace enforcement, especially in the South during the early 2000s,
was at odds with the demands for undocumented labor and practices
to employ undocumented workers. Raids across the South contributed
to the deepening construction of immigrant illegality in the New South
(Stuesse 2016). For Arturo, whose father lost his job at a poultry processing plant, the combination of workplace raids and the passage of HB 87,
the state's anti-immigrant bill, signaled to him that the state's orientation
toward undocumented immigrants was moving in a hostile direction.

During our interview in his parents' home in Athens, Omar echoed
Arturo's perception that workplace raids in Georgia and beyond created
a sense of fear and noticeably shifting dynamics in the community. He
shared,

> It was pretty rough at the beginning of 2007, 2008. There were many raids
> here. A lot of people were getting scared and actually leaving to go back
> to Mexico. When that time period, that's when my dad lost [his job], he
> couldn't renew his license, and he lost his good paying job and ever since
> then, he can't renew his license.

Omar's answer reveals the laissez-faire approach the state had taken toward undocumented immigrants, as his dad had a driver's license, which helped him work a job that paid well. In 2010, when his dad tried to renew his license to keep his job, he could not, which sent Omar's family into a state of financial precarity. Like Omar, Maya, who migrated at the age of nine in 2001, shared that when she migrated with her family so her parents could work in the chicken processing plants, "it was easier, I think, to get a license with just an ID. It was different. There were different laws; there wasn't as strict laws as there is now. So, it wasn't hard until maybe 2006–2007." Omar and Maya, as well as other undocumented young adults, felt like it was getting harder and harder to stay in Georgia through the 2000s as the state was becoming increasingly hostile. For example, Maya's older cousin, who was also undocumented, had been attending college and was able to pay in-state tuition. She shared:

> For him, it was much easier because back then, they didn't charge out-of-state tuition; as long as you lived in Georgia, everything was okay. But I think it was in 2009, I want to say, they started charging out-of-state tuition. I knew because he was talking to me about it, and that was when I realized things were going to be a little harder.

In stark contrast to the experiences of respondents in the Los Angeles area, the growth of the Latinx unauthorized community in the metropolitan Atlanta area created a more hostile climate for Latinx undocumented young adults and their families. While this backlash may be very similar to the anti-immigrant climate in California during the 1990s, the current trajectory of immigration laws and policies in the state suggests there will be little to no reprieve for undocumented immigrants in Georgia.

The divergent contexts of reception just described highlight how Latinx undocumented young adults experienced inclusion or exclusion in their home states and cities, a key part of their legal ecologies. Latinx undocumented young adults in the metropolitan Los Angeles area described the presence of co-ethnics, for example, other Latinxs, as integral to creating a sense of place. However, in Atlanta, the emergence of a sizable Latinx undocumented immigrant community created a backlash in the general population that impacted undocumented young people's sense of place or belonging. In both areas, Latinx undocumented young adults had to confront their legal status; paradoxically, in Los Angeles, the large presence of Latinx undocumented immigrants made this identity less salient in the day-to-day lives of respondents, particularly during childhood. In contrast, in Atlanta, the equation of being Latinx and undocumented resulted in a sense of being scrutinized. These different contexts also gave rise to differing experiences in the early years of Latinx undocumented young adults' school experiences.

The Formative Schooling Experiences of Latinx Undocumented Young Adults

The undocumented young adults I interviewed migrated to the United States between the ages of four months and fifteen years old, and their primary socializing experiences were in the public school system. The 1982 Supreme Court decision in *Plyler v. Doe* guarantees public school access for undocumented immigrants. The *Plyler* decision created a legally protected space for undocumented children based on the premise that denying them access to public education would create an educational underclass. Before the *Plyler* decision, though, in 1974, the Supreme Court decided in *Lau v. Nichols*[1] that teaching non-English speakers in a language they could not understand violated their right to equal educational opportunity (Faulstich et al. 1999). However, how immigrant children are educated is determined by schools, resulting in varied pedagogical approaches and practices, especially when educating newcomer students (Figueroa 2013; Faltis and Valdes 2010). Following the *Lau* decision, in 1976, California passed the Chacon-Moscone Bilingual Bicultural Education Act (1976), legislating that students "receive instruction in a language understandable to the student, which recognizes the pupil's primary language and teaches the pupil English" (Faulstich et al. 1999, 115). In the years following the *Lau* decision, California invested in building infrastructure for bilingual education, including training bilingual educators (Faulstich et al. 1999). Much of this was undone in 1998, when California voters passed Proposition 227, requiring that English language learners (ELLs) be taught primarily in English

---

1. *Lau v. Nichols*, 414 U.S. 563 (1974).

for one year before being placed in mainstream classes unless parents requested otherwise. Proposition 227, also called "English for the Children," reflected broader ideological debates about the racialization of language learning, including the value of the Spanish language and efforts to make English the official language of the United States (Rosa and Flores 2017; Galindo 1997). These same debates happened in Georgia as the Latinx immigrant population grew during the 1990s. By 1996, Georgia was one of eleven states in the U.S. South to pass English-only legislation, establishing English as the state's official language (Beck and Allexsaht-Snider 2002). In addition, three cities in the Atlanta metropolitan area passed local ordinances requiring that 75 percent of words on a commercial sign be in English (Beck and Allexsaht-Snider 2002). The xenophobia embedded in English-only policies influenced approaches to educating the growing bilingual population with an emphasis on English immersion. While some districts and schools seized the opportunity to integrate Spanish-speaking students and families, this was the exception and not the rule (Wainer 2006). Instead, while communities in the South acknowledged the economic value of Latinx immigrant labor, very little was invested in allocating resources and efforts toward integration, including robust ELL programs (Wainer 2006; Beck and Allexsaht-Snider 2002).

In both California and Georgia, participants described early feelings of apprehension and anxiety in school, primarily because it was a new environment, and they did not speak English. While the initial school experiences of young people were similar, certain important differences distinguished the formative schooling experiences of Latinx undocumented young adults in Los Angeles from those in Atlanta, reflecting the migration histories of these two metropolitan areas and, relatedly, the capacity, training, and experience of educators to work with immigrant students. Participants in Los Angeles described being placed in bilingual education classes, ELL classes, or having teachers who spoke Spanish, which eased the transition to school. A small minority of young people who migrated to the Atlanta area in the early 1990s reported that theirs was the only Latinx family in the community. They found the early school transition to be more difficult. Those who migrated a bit later described a small minority of Latinx students in their schools and few, if any, teachers who spoke Spanish. In both Los Angeles and Atlanta, participants' varied experiences in their early school interactions highlight the deeper sociopolitical dynamics of programs and practices focused on English language development for immigrant students (Figueroa 2013; Faltis and Valdes 2010). These early schooling experiences are also important to unpack because they were part of forming the foundation for later educational experiences, aspirations, and expectations.

Early Schooling Experiences in Los Angeles and Atlanta

Participants who grew up in the Los Angeles area attended schools that were predominantly Latinx, primarily because they migrated to communities that were also predominantly Latinx. This facilitated a smoother transition in school, in contrast with students who migrated to Atlanta, in two important ways. First, students in California described being in classrooms where they encountered not only other Latinx students but also Spanish-speaking teachers; this helped them feel more comfortable. Julieta, who migrated to the Los Angeles area from El Salvador when she was two years old, described how she learned English in the following way:

> When I came here, I didn't know English. But since I was little, I just picked up the language really fast. I don't even remember how I learned it or anything. I did, in elementary school, I did have Spanish-speaking teachers, which helped a lot. They were bilingual.

In Julieta's recollection of her elementary school experience, she was in regular classrooms with teachers who spoke both Spanish and English, facilitating an already rapid process of learning how to speak English. Similarly, Joshua, who migrated to the United States in 1994 and entered school before the passage of Proposition 227, started kindergarten that September; he shared:

> They put me into the all-Spanish class in kinder . . . I was scared. . . . And then after kindergarten, I went to bilingual classes; by second grade, I entered honors already. I made great progress. My first-grade teacher, she was a very, she was a great teacher from what I remember. . . . She always made us write a lot.

For Joshua, although he was scared to start school, entering an all-Spanish kindergarten followed by transitional bilingual classes helped him progress quickly. While most young people recounted experiences similar to those of Julieta and Joshua, Eduardo migrated as a teenager in 2006 and described a very different school experience. Despite moving to a community that he described as predominantly Hispanic, he shared: "High school was actually tough; I was a fifteen-year-old kid, not knowing any language and just getting tossed into math class. So that was weird and tough." As Eduardo describes, he was placed in a math class that was conducted primarily in English, making it challenging for him to acclimate. But this also reflected a shift in orientation toward bilingual learners following the passage of Proposition 227. These contrasting experiences highlight how schools in the metropolitan Los Angeles area, although equipped to work with Spanish-speaking undocumented students by offering English language development classes and bilingual courses, still had to work within the English-only framework by the 2000s. As Julieta's and Joshua's experiences demonstrate, bilingual classes and having teachers in elementary school who spoke Spanish and English sped along their English language learning, an experience reflected by many undocumented young people in the Los Angeles area. Perhaps highlighting the larger challenges facing bilingual education, especially in a post–Proposition 227 era, even in communities where the Latinx population was the majority, pressures to have students linguistically assimilate were pervasive.

Young people who grew up in the Los Angeles area also stated that they often did not talk about their status with other students when they were in school, most likely because they were children and may have been told by their parents not to talk about it. A reality reflected in a common phrase in the Latinx undocumented community, *no le digas a nadie*, or, "don't tell anyone." During interviews, they shared that there was a sense that many other people in their communities were also undocumented. Estefania explained: "Because throughout the whole school year, it [being undocumented] wasn't a problem, and no one really cared. Especially in L.A. because a lot of people are undocumented, so it's, I guess, it's common, and you don't really talk about it." Mirelsa's tourist visa expired while she was in middle school, and she graduated from a large public high school in downtown Los Angeles: "I guess we didn't really talk about being undocumented. . . . I knew some people who were also undocumented, but we didn't talk about it on a regular basis." While respondents said that they did not discuss their status in part to protect themselves and their families, there was also a sense in Los Angeles that their status did not matter for their *early* schooling experiences—primarily because, as Latinx children, they did not stand out in their schools.

In contrast, participants who migrated to the Atlanta area often migrated to communities that were either predominantly Black or predominantly white, reflective of Georgia's new immigrant destination status. Manuel migrated to the United States with his family when he was three years old to join his father, who had been living in California. His family lived on the edge of Santa Barbara County, about two hours north of Los Angeles. They lived there for eight years before moving to Atlanta. Manuel shared during our interview that when he first started school in Atlanta, he was placed back in sixth grade, although he should have started seventh grade. He shared,

> It was very different, very different from California. In California, I remember I was in sixth grade. When I came over here, they put me back in sixth grade. Over there [in California], they did a test first, see where my English was and everything, did I need anything, special classes to work on English, and stuff like that.

Manuel's transition to school in Atlanta was shaped in part by starting in middle school, where the school day shifts from a single classroom to multiple classes, and the fact that his family moved from a relatively small community on the Central Coast of California to urban Atlanta. However, I sensed in our interview that he expected a more welcoming space based on his experience in California and the prevalence of Latinx students in his community. He shared that he did not expect to start school the day his mom went to register him, but the school said he could start that day, and he remembered being unprepared. He shared:

> So, I was there. I don't know anybody. I don't know nothing. I don't even know how to get to the next class. . . . That was very . . . it was very scary, the first day of school. I didn't know which bus to get onto. Luckily, some teachers helped me out to get on the right bus. Then the school bus was . . . all the kids, I didn't know none of the kids. It was very different.

Revealing the nuances of racial dynamics in the "Nuevo South," Manuel described his community as predominantly Black when he and his family first moved there. As he moved through school, he watched the Latinx community grow. Much like young people in Los Angeles and similar to his own experience before moving to Atlanta, he eventually made friends with more Latinxs. Those who migrated to more suburban areas described experiences like Alondra's:

> The first school that I enrolled in . . . was in basically an all-white, pretty affluent community. That was helpful for learning English because I didn't have a lot of people to talk Spanish with, so it forced me to . . . I was on survival mode.

Early school experiences varied by the demographics of the community that participants moved to but generally reflected the emergence of Atlanta as a new immigration destination. Andres, who started third grade in Atlanta, shared that:

> When they put me in school, I was only speaking Spanish, but on, after the first day of school, I had already learned some English, and I brought it home, and my dad heard me speak English, and he got mad; he's like 'don't speak English in the house,' and my mom is like 'let him speak English, he has to learn' [laughing].

Andres did learn English quickly and, by middle school, was reading at a high school level. Despite his rapid growth, he was placed in English as a Second Language (ESL) classes through middle school. He shared, "Even though I spoke English pretty well, even all throughout middle school, they put me in ESL. But I was reading at a high school level by the time I was in middle school. I feel like they were just assuming that my English wasn't as good because I was Hispanic." Andres's experience shows that, although, over time, schools in the Atlanta area adapted to the new student population by offering English language development classes, racialized assumptions about the Latinx community kept Andres in ELL classes for much longer than needed. His experience also reflects a lack of understanding of the variability in English language development. Keeping Andres in ELL classes through middle school did not meet his academic needs. It should be noted that few, if any, young people described early school experiences that sought to reinforce the maintenance of their native language, Spanish.

The experiences of Manuel, Alondra, and Andres show how, during the late 1990s through the early 2000s, Atlanta was adjusting to the growth in the Latinx immigrant population. While the young people who grew up in Atlanta during this early period experienced these adjustments firsthand through their early school experiences, they were also learning what it meant to be undocumented by watching their parents navigate daily life. This was the case for young people in both Los Angeles and Atlanta. Additionally, as they got older, they began to understand that, as a group, growing up in the United States insulated them from some, but not all, of the discrimination their parents faced and would continue to face.

Understanding Racist Nativism through Their Parents' Eyes

The immigration histories and development of California and Georgia significantly shaped the early schooling experiences of the undocumented young people I interviewed. These same factors had impacts beyond school. Many, but not all, of the young people I got to know in these areas were very close to their families, and while they were growing up, they witnessed the discrimination their parents faced. Since they were children, they did not always think they would face the same treatment later in life, but they did begin to develop nascent understandings of the race-based exclusion to which undocumented immigrants were subject. Scholars have referred to this treatment as *racist nativism*, a racial ideology that relies on both racism—the belief in the superiority of the white race in the United States—and nativism—the belief in the superiority of "native-born" individuals over "non-natives." (Perez Huber et al. 2008). Undocumented young people in Atlanta described more acute experiences of racist nativism primarily because of the perception by the white population in the region of rapidly shifting demographics. The relatively accommodating social context of Los Angeles and, conversely, the hostile context of Atlanta, tell one story about how laws and policies impact

Latinx undocumented young adults. Young people in Los Angeles and Atlanta articulated acute feelings of discrimination as they transitioned out of high school and faced more barriers and challenges, especially related to college access. (I explore this in depth in the next chapter.) But the sociopolitical climate of each state translated to different everyday experiences of discrimination for Latinx undocumented young adults long before they transitioned out of high school. While Latinx undocumented young adults described personal experiences of discrimination primarily within the context of education, I found that witnessing their parents' experiences of discrimination also had profound impacts on their understandings of racist nativism toward Latinx undocumented immigrants.

Mateo, who migrated to Atlanta in the late 1990s at the age of ten, noted that his undocumented status "didn't kick in, nor did it matter because, after 9/11, that's when really I guess being an immigrant or undocumented really was more highlighted than before." While Mateo connected 9/11 to an increase in hostility toward undocumented immigrants, his status did not really matter to him until he turned sixteen:

> Well, I didn't really have a sense of what it was being undocumented or anything, and then at sixteen, everybody was getting their driver's license. At that point, that's when I started to understand that I didn't have that privilege. So, I guess most immigrants, undocumented students, or people start to realize that there is a difference, you know, but I think that around sixteen is when I started to understand.

Mateo's story is not that different from the common narrative of the undocumented youth experience that has been well-documented (Gonzales 2016; Abrego 2008; Enriquez 2015). Nevertheless, later in our interview, Mateo shared that, as living in Georgia became more difficult, he wrestled with feelings of shame about being Mexican because of the messages he was receiving from the media and the larger society: "I always felt proud of my father, proud of my mother. But with society, it was getting harder and harder to retain that pride. And there were times when I would feel guilty and feel embarrassed." Like Mateo, undocumented young adults growing up in the Atlanta area experienced the proliferation of restrictive laws in the 2000s primarily through the experiences of their parents, resulting at times in feelings of shame or embarrassment.

Marco, who migrated to South Atlanta in 2007 at the age of seven with his mother, explained that growing up, he "knew he was different," but it was not until middle school that he put "one and one together and realized that I was undocumented, and what came with that term." As Marco elaborated during our interview, his early experiences of what it meant to be undocumented were informed by his parents' experiences working in a factory and the way they were treated:

> My mom always said that she encountered a lot of racism, a lot of peo-
> ple discriminated against her based on her status, and the fact that she
> couldn't speak English too well. My dad, he was very quiet, he kept to
> himself, but he never expressed that, but he pointed out many injustices
> in our community in the way we were treated. . . . So, I was able to put
> one and one and was able to say I'm undocumented and undocumented
> people are treated a certain way, just from my mom's and dad's experience.

While Marco later learned that his undocumented status would make it difficult for him to attend college in-state, an experience he connected to a larger context of discrimination, his parents' experiences shaped his earliest experiences.

During separate interviews, sisters Araceli and Diana, who migrated to Norcross, a Latinx suburb of Atlanta, in 2003, relayed the same story to me. Responding to a question about whether they believed Georgia was a welcoming place for immigrants and about their own experiences of discrimination because of their status, Araceli said:

> This is probably the weirdest story you will ever hear. I remember one time
> my dad had ordered a GPS, I think. It was from Walmart. To pick it up, he
> needed an ID. I went with him. He showed them his passport from Mexico
> and not from here. He doesn't have any type of ID here. . . . They made the
> biggest deal about it. I remember sitting there. I was about, I want to say,
> fourteen. They were so rude to him. . . . I remember I just turned around.
> I wanted to cry because it hurts when it's your dad and you're seeing that
> happen to your dad.

While relaying this story, Araceli became very emotional and started to cry. Diana had a similar reaction, as her most vivid memory of the experience was seeing her father as vulnerable for the first time in her life. Like most undocumented immigrant children, Diana and Araceli had been protected from anti-immigrant sentiment, in part because they were children but also because their parents worked very hard to create a "normal childhood" for them and to shield them from the hostility that was growing in the state. Diana stated during our interview:

> I remember my dad had just, like, hanging low and just feeling so vulnerable at the moment. That someone, he, it wasn't outright spoken that he was undocumented, but by not having that Georgia state license, it was just assumed. . . . And to see him in that vulnerable moment. They always protected me from the discrimination. Sorry, I'm just getting teary-eyed now thinking about it because he was just in a very vulnerable, weak spot and I know he was, in a sense, ashamed, really.

During interviews, respondents recounted different variations of these painful experiences as they watched their parents endure exploitation, mistreatment, and discrimination. For Jasmin, it was a visit to a doctor who told her mother that, after sixteen years in the United States, she should know how to speak English. Jasmin shared that "even going to the bank, people [were] rude to [her] parents." While undocumented young adults in Georgia were not able to fully appreciate the impact of their status until they graduated from high school and aspired to go to college, their parents' experiences of discrimination shaped their perception of what it meant to be undocumented and influenced their sense of belonging.

In contrast, Latinx undocumented young adults who grew up in California described a policy climate that provided them with an increased sense of security about their own and their parents' safety. For undocumented young adults in both Los Angeles and Atlanta, driving posed the greatest risk. While I was conducting interviews and doing fieldwork in California, there was an important legislative reform that signaled to respondents that California was indeed a welcoming state. In January 2015, AB 60 granted driver's licenses to undocumented immigrants. While many respondents already had driver's licenses because they were DACA recipients, Latinx undocumented young adults discussed this law as providing protection for their parents and eliciting a greater sense of safety and comfort. Joshua, who was one of the few respondents in both California and Georgia to not yet have DACA, commented:

> I just got my license two weeks ago through AB 60. That is a big stress reliever. . . . So there is a lot of things that are going through your mind while you're driving, and you just want to get home. You just want to get from point A to point B and just be safe. And you never know in the middle of your travel, you'll get stopped.

The announcement of AB 60 created a huge sense of relief for respondents in California because of the danger of driving while undocumented. Like Joshua, who felt great personal relief because he could now legally drive, other respondents in California shared a similar sense of relief, but for their parents. Yosimar stated: "My mom and my dad are trying to get their license with AB 60." Aurora reflected during our interview on the emotional weight lifted by being able to get a driver's license:

> I thought about this two weeks ago, and I started crying because my mom and my dad don't have the DACA thing. They haven't done the AB 60, because they haven't had the time to go . . . because they're busy with work. For me, just thinking about the fact that my mom drives from where we live here to pick me up on Fridays or for anything, I'm like, "She's putting herself at risk," and not a small risk . . . this could lead to really bad things.

For Aurora, the prospect of her parents eventually getting their driver's licenses made her feel better about them going about their everyday lives and created a sense of safety for the Latinx undocumented young adults living in the state. Again, this policy change, in conjunction with the lack of stigma in their local communities associated with being Latinx and undocumented, reduced young people's acute fears for their parents. Although AB 60 was a recent legislative reform, respondents from Los Angeles did convey a stronger sense of belonging because of the presence of other Latinxs and shifts in the state toward more accommodating policies. Unlike the respondents in Georgia, where there was a trend toward further exclusion, respondents in California observed a trend toward inclusion.

Conclusion

The childhood experiences of Latinx undocumented young adults profoundly shaped their understanding of what it meant to be undocumented. It was during these early years that young people's legal ecologies were taking shape. In the Los Angeles area, the locale's history as a traditional immigrant destination provided a sense of comfort for young people, as participants described communities that felt ethnoracially similar to the countries they migrated from, including hearing Spanish spoken. In Atlanta, participants described being among the first or one of a few Latinx families to move to their communities. In both locales, broader public debates about English shaped their formative schooling experiences. In the Los Angeles and Orange County areas, young people described entering schools that were more prepared to offer bilingual education, including teachers who spoke Spanish. In Atlanta, those who entered school in the late 1990s through early 2000s described being in classrooms where teachers did not speak Spanish and, in some cases, young people having to serve as translators themselves. For many, but not all, because of their age at migration, they learned English quickly. Still, it should be noted that none of the young people in California or Georgia discussed formative school experiences when they were encouraged to maintain their native language, Spanish. During their early childhoods, these undocumented young people were also developing a sense of the legal precarity associated with being undocumented by observing their parents' experiences.

While undocumented young people generally described a sense of security within the context of their families, the legal vulnerability created by U.S. immigration law made day-to-day life challenging. For many, it was during their childhoods that shifting sociopolitical dynamics, with California becoming increasingly welcoming and Georgia becoming increasingly hostile, started to take shape. During childhood, participants described an awareness of the limitations of their parents' undocumented status, not unlike what U.S.-born children of undocumented immigrants experience. However, the impact of undocumented status on their daily lives and future goals was just starting to come into view. As undocumented young people began to transition into their later high school years, the focus of the next chapter, they began to see how their legal status would shape their educational trajectories and life goals.

CHAPTER 3

PATHWAYS TO COLLEGE IN NEW AND OLD DESTINATIONS

Both Melanie and Jennifer were college-bound during high school. Melanie attended a large public high school in a suburb of Atlanta, Georgia. Jennifer also attended a large public high school in a Los Angeles, California suburb. Both made themselves competitive for college by taking advanced placement classes, preparing for college entrance exams, and participating in extracurricular activities. Both were not only "college-ready," they were also competitive college applicants. Yet when I interviewed each, only one was enrolled in college. Melanie had recently quit her job at McDonald's. She was applying to colleges for the third year in a row, hoping to get accepted to a college in the Atlanta area with financial assistance. During our interview, she recounted her experience of starting the college application process to attend the University of Georgia, where, given her grades, she would have qualified for a scholarship for high-achieving students living in the state. As Melanie and her twin sister were navigating the college application process, they came across what they initially thought was a glitch in the application system:

> You're not even allowed to apply or anything. So my sister . . . she called the office, the admissions office, and was like, "I'm trying to send in my application, it's not working, I don't know what happened." And then they asked her things . . . they started asking her like, "what did you put?" And

then she told them, "Oh well, I put that I don't have status." And then . . . that's when they told us like, "Oh well, you can't apply." And that's when we started researching what can we really do, and we found out that we can't apply to these schools and basically, we can't get in-state tuition here. . . . It was like finding out all our college options were just not going to be possible at all.

In contrast, Jennifer grew up in the Los Angeles area and was a sophomore at a competitive public four-year university in Southern California. While she initially faced challenges during the college and financial aid application process, she shared that the passage of Assembly Bill (AB) 131, also known as the California Dream Act, offering state and institutional financial aid, was integral to her college-going journey. She shared:

In my junior year [of high school], second semester, the California Dream Act gets announced, it passed. I didn't believe it. I thought, why would they give money for us to go to school? . . . I don't know, I just didn't believe it. I didn't think tuition was going to get covered. My AVID [Advancement Via Individual Determination] teacher told me to research this college and my AP [Advanced Placement] teachers. I said they [California] are not going to cover X amount of dollars. That's too much money. Even though I still thought they're not going to cover everything, I knew there was a little bit of hope. That little bit of push for hope that I had is what me got me through.

As both Melanie and Jennifer describe, for undocumented young people, state-level college access policies have real consequences and symbolic implications for their motivation to continue to navigate the journey to college. Melanie's college dreams were deflated when she learned she was barred from applying to the University of Georgia and would have to pay out-of-state tuition at any public college. At the same time, Jennifer was buoyed by the passage of in-state financial aid.

Each year, approximately 98,000 undocumented students graduate from high school (Zong and Batalova 2019). While the United States Supreme Court held in *Plyler v. Doe* (1982) that undocumented children have a right to a public education through twelfth grade, their futures are more uncertain after high school (Gonzales 2011; Abrego 2006). As discussed in chapter 1, access to postsecondary education is left up to individual states, resulting in a policy landscape that is as complex as it is contradictory. For undocumented students, like many college-bound students, attending college hinges on whether you can pay. Laws or policies that offer in-state tuition *and* state financial aid provide the ideal situation for undocumented students. As of 2021, thirty states offer in-state tuition to eligible undocumented students through various mechanisms. Seventeen states, including California, have codified in-state tuition to eligible undocumented immigrants through state legislation.

Meanwhile, seven other state university systems (including governing bodies like a board of regents) extend in-state tuition to eligible undocumented immigrants. In five states, in-state tuition is offered only to Deferred Action for Childhood Arrivals (DACA) holders. Eleven states provide state financial aid to undocumented students, and several other states allow institutional or private aid. In contrast, six states, including Georgia, either explicitly ban undocumented immigrants from attending public universities or require that undocumented immigrants pay out-of-state tuition, making public higher education practically impossible to access. Unlike some other states, Georgia bans undocumented young people from its most competitive colleges (Trivette and English 2017). Finally, many states do not have a state policy for undocumented immigrant students, effectively leaving young people in these states with no guidance for attending college. While states that actively exclude undocumented immigrants comprise a much smaller share than states that offer in-state tuition and/or financial aid, the consequences for undocumented young adults living in these states are significant. In this chapter, I unpack the influence of this complex college access landscape on the educational experiences and pathways of Latinx undocumented young adults in Los Angeles and Atlanta as they were approaching the end of high school and embarking on their college-going journeys.

The Legal Ecologies of College Choice: College Access for Undocumented Students

The period of adolescence and emerging adulthood is a crucial time for all young people as they develop a story about a future self or a future orientation. *Future orientation* is the "image individuals have about their future . . . a personal subjective story that gives meaning to one's life" (Seginer 2008, 272). The concept of future orientation is applicable here for understanding how the young people in this study confronted and engaged with the challenges they realized they would face as they transitioned out of high school and what it meant for their unfolding futures. As we learned in chapter 2, young people in both Los Angeles and Atlanta described early school experiences marked by relatively short, but not uneventful, transition periods from English language learner programs to mainstream classrooms. While participants in Southern California entered schools more equipped to work with Spanish-speaking students than participants who migrated to Atlanta, both groups of young people successfully navigated the transition from elementary and middle school into high school. Once in high school, participants described educational experiences they perceived as like those of their U.S.-born peers. More importantly, they described a desire and demonstrated the potential to attend college. Most participants grew up in under-resourced communities where navigating the road to college is fraught. They encountered many of the same structural barriers college-aspiring first-generation Latinx youth face—uncertainty about how to pay for college and varying degrees of guidance and encouragement from high school counselors and teachers.

In the United States, a college degree is a tool for social mobility and a cultural norm (Goyette 2008). For immigrant youth, including undocumented youth, the weight of college expectations may be heavier as they carry their parents' migration hopes and dreams with them throughout their schooling experience (Louie 2012; Smith 2006). Research shows that children of immigrants and young people who are immigrants themselves strive to do well in school and attend college to repay their immigrant parents' sacrifice. This phenomenon is referred to as "keeping the immigrant bargain" (Loiue 2012; Smith 2006). While the concept suggests a rational-choice perspective on immigrant educational attainment. For the participants in this study, their motivation to attend college was also deeply emotional, as parents' migration experiences and sacrifices fostered aspirational capital (Acevedo-Gil 2017; Yosso 2005). A childhood spent watching their parents work hard and experience discrimination strengthened their commitment to creating a better life through educational mobility. Undocumented young adults in both lo-cales described a desire to keep the immigrant bargain by attending college. The opportunity to fulfill this bargain was directly mediated by state laws and policies governing college access and financial aid. When laws and policies were exclusionary, as is the case in Georgia, the desire to keep the immigrant bargain inspired activism, something I explore in-depth in chapter 5. Despite policy challenges, participants in both Los Angeles and Atlanta were highly motivated to go to college. These aspira-tions were further reinforced by the "college for all" ethos that permeates American high schools (Goyette 2008; Rosenbaum 2001).

Regardless of where they lived, participants began to confront chal-lenges navigating the road to college in high school, the most critical period in the journey. College attendance is the outcome of a multistage process that higher education scholars identify as the *college choice pro-cess* (Acevedo-Gil 2017; Perez and McDonough 2008; Perna 2006; Hoss-ler and Gallagher 1987). Emerging in the late 1980s, the college choice model outlines three stages in the college-going process: the predisposi-tion stage, the search process, and ultimately the choice process (Hoss-ler and Gallagher 1987). During the predisposition stage, typically from sixth to tenth grade, students develop an interest in college and begin to articulate aspirations and expectations (Domina et al. 2011; Hossler and Gallagher 1987). During the search stage, occurring from tenth through twelfth grade, students identify colleges to apply to. Finally, during the choice stage, typically during twelfth grade, students consider their of-fers and decide where to attend. While this multistage model provides a starting point for understanding the college choice process, research shows this process is qualitatively different for Latinx students, includ-ing undocumented students (Rosales 2024; Acevedo-Gil 2017; Perez and McDonough 2008; Perna 2006). For example, as discussed, Latinx students draw aspirational capital from their parents while also seek-ing information about college from others, including extended family networks and older peers (Perez and McDonough 2008). Even as Lat-inx students seek information about college from older family members and peers, institutional agents remain a crucial influence, facilitating movement toward or away from college (Perez and McDonough 2008; Stanton-Salazar 2001). For example, sociologist Roberta Espinoza (2011) describes pivotal moments as generally positive interventions by educators in the lives of college-aspiring working-class youth. These pivotal moments can set young people on the path to college, as happened for Jennifer, whom we met at this chapter's beginning. A high school college preparation program teacher helped Jennifer understand that, while it may be challenging to attend college, the legislative landscape in California provided her with "a strategy." In contrast, young people in Georgia were less comfortable sharing their status with teachers and counselors and, therefore, had fewer opportunities to experience pivotal moments that set them on the path to college, highlighting the added layer of disclosure management undocumented young people must navigate during the college choice process (Rosales 2024; Muñoz 2015).

The sociopolitical context shaped the nature and contours of the structural challenges participants faced as they transitioned out of high school, and the implications for the perception and reality of their developing futures. This was much more pronounced for undocumented young adults in the Atlanta area because of the Board of Regents policies. For most of the young people in Atlanta, learning about the limitations of their status derailed their educational trajectories for varying periods of time. In the Los Angeles area, even after years of state-level college access laws (e.g., AB 540), participants described inconsistent levels of support during the college application process. Once in college, they had to overcome various challenges to have a similar experience to their U.S.-born peers. In both locales, young people's ability to plan long-term for their futures in the United States was constrained by the absence of a pathway to citizenship, even with the introduction of DACA.

Constructing Possible Futures in California

In October 2001, California Governor Gray Davis signed AB 540, which allowed eligible undocumented youth to pay in-state tuition at California public colleges and universities. Even with in-state tuition, research has been focused heavily on the challenges undocumented college students face on the road to and through college (Enriquez 2011; Gonzales 2011; Abrego and Gonzales 2010). While AB 540 eased the transition out of high school for college-bound undocumented students, the primary challenge remained how to pay for college once they were enrolled.

Before the introduction of AB 130 and AB 131, a pair of laws together known as the California Dream Act, offering state-level financial aid and institutional aid (financial support from public colleges and universities), the educational pathways of undocumented young adults were marked by stops and starts and working long hours. Julieta, who was born in El Salvador and lived there with her grandparents until she was two years old, was enrolled in a public four-year college in Southern California when I first interviewed her in 2010. She described how, in 2008, when she graduated from high school, nearly seven years after AB 540 was passed, but before the California Dream Act, she and her high school counselors did not fully understand how to navigate the path to college. More importantly, Julieta did not know how she would afford college without financial aid. Reflecting on understanding the implications of her undocumented status, Julieta shared,

> But the thing is, I didn't even realize how, I guess, critical the situation was. Until high school, when I was applying for college . . . I knew I had been born someplace else but so had other people. Once it came to applying for colleges, I was so happy because I thought I'm going to receive financial aid; because my parents don't make that much money and everything. So, I'm going to be able to do everything that I want. And I realized that I couldn't, and it was kind of devastating.

While AB 540 made it possible for Julieta to attend a prestigious public university, her journey through college was marked by periods of worrying about how she would pay for college, a common experience for undocumented college students in California prior to the passage of the California Dream Act. Before 2013, undocumented young people enrolled in college described hustling for scholarships, working twenty to forty hours per week, or taking quarters and semesters off to save to pay for future enrollment, a practice known as "stopping out."

The implementation of DACA in 2012, in conjunction with the passage of the California Dream Act, expanded the educational pathways of undocumented students. In 2013, after years of activism by undocumented youth in the state, the California Dream Act was signed into law, granting state and institutional aid to eligible undocumented immigrants. This shift in policy significantly impacted the trajectories of college-bound undocumented young adults. As Jennifer shared at the beginning of the chapter, the passage of the California Dream Act offered a sense of "hope" and made it seem possible for her to attend college. Because Jennifer had gone through a low point during her sophomore year in high school, a "depression phase" where she started to realize that trying to go to college was going to be a big challenge, when the California Dream Act was enacted, she was wary about how much financial aid she would receive because she did not believe that the public would want to financially support undocumented immigrants like herself. When it came time for Jennifer to apply to college, she applied to various campuses in the University of California and California State University systems and navigated a confusing financial path to a decision to attend a University of California campus in Southern California, close to home.

The change in law created a new category of students, California Dream Act students, who needed guidance about applying for financial aid and understanding their financial aid packages once they were admitted. Like Jennifer, Alejandra, who was enrolled at a University of California campus, had a similarly confusing process after getting accepted to three California State Universities, two University of California campuses, and three private liberal arts colleges. As Alejandra's classmates were getting their letters of acceptance and financial aid offers, Alejandra realized she "wasn't getting anything." By this, she meant that she was not receiving financial aid. Her counselor told her, "Oh, well that happens when you're AB 540." Alejandra was not aware of what AB 540 was and asked her counselor to explain. Her counselor elaborated:

> She's like, "Oh, AB 540 is like whether you qualify for money to go to college if you've been three years in high school and you graduated from a California. . . ." She was just explaining everything. I was like, "Oh, then I do qualify." She's like, "Yeah, but what happens is that they distribute the money to everyone else, and they leave the Dream Act for last, so you might not get a lot of money." I was like, "Oh, no." She said, "What happens in this case is you should try to go to a community college." I was like, "No, I have good grades to go to another school." People were telling me, "You're not going to be able to go. There's no way they're going to give you money. You're AB 540."

Alejandra was discouraged by her classmates, and more importantly, by her guidance counselor, an institutional agent who should have helped her navigate the financial aid process with more certainty. After learning more about her AB 540 status, Alejandra figured out the California Dream Act application on her own. She shared, "I think I did it by myself. I don't know how, but I did." She was the first one in her school to get the California Dream Act and, as other students learned about Alejandra applying, they started to approach her and ask for help. "A lot of people who I never would have thought were undocumented were undocumented. . . . Everybody who was undocumented went up to me like, 'She [her counselor] told me to go up to you because you already filled it [the Dream Act application] out." When the acceptance letter and financial aid offer came from the college she ultimately enrolled in, Alejandra could not believe it. Between getting in-state tuition through AB 540 and the Cal Grant, the cost of college was fully covered her first year. Alejandra's counselor, though, was pessimistic about the offer, telling her, "That's not possible." Alejandra called the financial aid office to confirm that she understood the financial aid offer, and when it was confirmed, she was thrilled.

Like Alejandra, once admitted, young people in California described confusion over how much financial support they were getting and, at times, little to no transparency about their financial aid. Xavier, who grew up in the Pomona Valley, had attended community college for four years before he was able to transfer. He had been accepted to his dream college, a University of California campus. Initially he was not sure whether he would be able to go because his financial aid offer was unclear. But he was determined to save the money he needed to attend. As he described,

> I was finally able to get on the [financial aid] portal. Then I saw the numbers. It was really confusing. I just remember seeing, like, "I need $5,000 by the time I get there. By the time I get accepted to attend [a UC campus]." I was like, "Whoa, I need to come up with $5,000 in two months or three months" so I was working almost three jobs because I wasn't sure if it was going to be covered.

Xavier, like many undocumented young adults, was a member of a low-income family. To cover the potential $5,000 he might be expected to pay, he continued working his retail job and started to work a second job at a warehouse. He said, "I was basically on my feet all day, just running around." After several phone calls to the financial aid office, Xavier learned he would only be responsible for $2,500 of his educational costs that year. While that was more manageable than the $5,000 he thought he would have to pay, it was still a large amount for Xavier. He did, however, work enough to cover the $2,500 and to save some money for emergency expenses, which was reassuring because he would be far from his family who lived in Southern California. During our interview, I sensed that Xavier continued to worry about having money to pay for college. He shared that he planned to work again in retail over the summer: "Right now, I'm just hoping that, financially, it's going continue to cover it. I am looking for a summer job just in case there is a percentage of it that I do have to pay."

Like Xavier, other participants worried about paying for college each year, but they also had to develop strategies to manage the money they received from financial aid. Luz, who decided not to work to focus completely on school, had to make the $1,600 remaining from her package of financial assistance last a whole semester, including paying for housing. While Luz had been estranged from her father growing up, they reconnected when she was fifteen. Although they had a complicated relationship, she decided to reach out and ask for his help because she found herself running out of money. She said, "You know what, I need your help. . . . I need money. I don't care if it's little. You're responsible for me; you weren't there for my other years. Now is the time that I really need you." Luz's father supported her with $200 per month and, as Luz shared: "It helps pay my monthly utilities, my phone bill, gas, groceries." In addition, her mom sent her $100 to $200 every two weeks. While Luz was aware that her financial situation was challenging, she did share that she felt "very fortunate. I know it's harder for me. I know I have it tougher than other kids, but I know other kids have it tougher than me." Similarly, Miriam received three different institutional scholarships, which covered her tuition and housing, and left her with about $1,000 for ten weeks of living expenses. As a result, each quarter was a financial and personal struggle for her. She joked that she survived by eating "a lot of Top Ramen." In her first year, she explained that, although she did not have to pay anything out-of-pocket for college, financial stress was a defining part of her college experience. While this experience may not seem very different from that of any low-income student, Miriam connected her financial stresses in college to both her own and her parents' precarious legal status. During our interview, I learned that she occasionally sent money home to her family, and this was due in part to her parents' periods of unemployment. While Miriam appreciated the opportunity to be in college, she was at times constrained by her status from fully participating in college life. This included being unable to take trips with friends or secure certain internships. While she could accept these experiences as minor inconveniences, she also pointed out during our interview that she changed the course of her career plans because of her status and could not get the types of internship experiences she needed to pursue her career goals:

> My dream has always been to be able to represent the U.S. in another nation. I've always really wanted to do that. The issue with that is I can't get internships to get any experience for that because I need to be a citizen. Even with DACA . . . I have to be a citizen, and I can't be a citizen. Whenever I do find an internship that is working for the government, it's always I can't do it because I can't go, I don't have the money for it, I don't have the citizenship status for it.

Other participants expressed a desire to work for the government but were also acutely aware that their lack of citizenship status precluded them from realizing their goals. Eduardo, for example, had graduated from college and was enrolled in a master's degree program in mechanical engineering. While he was happy to be pursuing a graduate degree, he decided to attend graduate school only after he was let go from an internship in aerospace engineering, which required citizenship. In retrospect, Eduardo had a good sense of humor about this situation. Still, his answers revealed that his career goal was to work in aerospace engineering, and he only changed course because of his legal status. During our interview, he recounted preparing himself to leave the internship if they asked him to:

> Yeah, I was like, whatever, if they say go home, then I'll just go home [laughs]. So, I was doing my thing and I get a call at human resources and

I go to HR and they said, "Give us your badge and you're not allowed at the
facility." So, I wasn't allowed back in the facility. That sucked.

While Eduardo was pragmatic about his dismissal and implied that he
was expecting it, he had to change his career pathway and instead pursue
mechanical engineering. Eduardo may have handled the dismissal better
than one might expect because he had other options, including attending
graduate school, as indeed he did. Unlike Latinx undocumented young
adults in Georgia, access to a college education allowed Eduardo to continue to pursue his larger goals, although he also had to let go of some of
his original plans for his future.

Constructing Possible Futures in Georgia

At age twenty-six, Mateo was one of the older participants I interviewed
in Atlanta and was therefore old enough to experience and remember
a noticeable shift in the reception of Latinx immigrants in Georgia. He
migrated to Atlanta from Mexico with his sister and his aunt around
1997. While his memory was fuzzy about the exact year, he distinctly
remembered that he was in third grade. Mateo and his sister, who is two
years older, were reunited with their parents, who had been living in the
Atlanta area for about a year. Mateo was about twelve when September 11, 2001, happened, and it was then that he noticed that "being an
immigrant or undocumented was more highlighted than before." Then,
when Mateo turned sixteen and wanted to get his driver's license along
with his U.S.-born friends, when he learned he was not going to be able
to get a license, he began to understand the ramifications of his status,
including for his hopes of going to college. He described feeling ashamed
that he could not get his license and also starting to realize that it would
be very challenging, if not impossible, to pursue other goals, like going
to college. He described feeling like "there was no sense in me trying
to utilize my knowledge for college because it's not really something I
can . . ." and as Mateo trailed off during our interview, he shared that at
twenty-six, he realized that he was naïve about his status at age sixteen.
While Mateo shared that in retrospect, he could have gone on to get
good grades and graduate from high school, his decisions at the time

were influenced by the political context in which he was living. As he shared during our interview, he got high scores on exams in school and on the SAT. Instead, he dropped out of high school because he believed that because of his legal status, he was not entitled to opportunities like going to college. During our interview, he elaborated,

> And like teachers would tell me, "Man, there are people throwing money for people like you [smart students] to go to school," and to me, it was like, "Ah, but the thing is, I'm undocumented." Well, I didn't think of myself as undocumented; back in those days, I thought of myself as illegal.

For Mateo, coming of age during the rise of anti-immigrant hostility in Georgia significantly shaped his view of himself and what he could accomplish. The distinction between thinking of himself as undocumented versus "illegal" reflected how he internalized the anti-immigrant discourse that was rampant in Georgia, and this discourse had significant implications for his educational trajectory. As he astutely observed, the laws and policies passed in Georgia had important implications for individual's behavior, including his own:

> One thing I could say just right off is that when you take hope away from individuals, I think that you are prone to get extreme behavior, whether it's depression, somewhere along that line, or just, I guess, willing to do whatever it takes. So, I guess the key is to finding that energy and channeling it the right, and appropriate way, for me.

Despite the educational obstacles he encountered, when I interviewed Mateo in a lively Mexican restaurant, he had earned his GED and was attending Freedom University (FU), a community-based educational organization offering weekly college-level classes and support for the college application process to undocumented young people in the Atlanta-Athens area. Still, at twenty-six, he was unsure whether he would ever attend college.

Reflecting on her high school experience, Belen, who migrated with her family to the Atlanta metropolitan area in 2000, shared that, in middle school, she was placed in gifted classes, setting her on a college-bound path. When she got to high school, she started to take advanced placement courses and planned to attend college. As she moved into her sophomore and junior years of high school, she started to learn that her status might prevent her from attending college. Belen, who attended high school in a community she described as "upper-middle-class," shared that her parents deliberately chose that community because the schools were some of the best in the county, but the school was predominantly African American and white. She noted that the Hispanic population was definitely a part of the student body, sharing that there were at least five or six other Latinxs in her advanced placement classes. During her junior year of high school, Belen learned about the ban and, in her words, "kind of" approached her counselors. But as she went on to share, "But at that time, I kind of also knew. I was a lot more informed about my status. So, I felt like I kinda knew the reality. I felt like my high school counselors ain't really going to help me, so I didn't approach them about that." This hunch was confirmed when, at a mandatory graduate meeting, Belen decided to ask her counselors for help:

> We had a mandatory meeting with [a] counselor to make sure that we were up to date with our graduation requirements and everything. And I kinda just told them. I was like, "Oh, so I'm undocumented, and I don't really know what my options for college are." And they didn't really know what to tell me. They were like, "Well, I'm not really sure; I think you should go online and research that." . . . So, I just kind of expected that too, so that's why I wasn't really open about it, especially with like my administrators or counselors or anything like that. I kind of knew that they weren't going to be able to, to help me with that.

Because Belen attended a high school that was predominantly African American and white, she did not feel comfortable revealing her status to administrators, counselors, or institutional agents who should have been able to help her navigate the college-going process. Belen thought that if she had attended a school with more Latinx students, she might have felt more comfortable sharing her status to help with college-going:

> I'm not really sure, I think just the fact that I didn't even feel really comfortable telling them that. I kinda just pretended like I would ask on a different

pretense, like "Oh I'm interested on this about scholarships about this." I didn't even really feel comfortable approaching them about being undocumented or my status or anything. So I didn't; I didn't feel like they were that open with it. And there wasn't any like, I feel, it's important when like at other schools where they have like maybe a larger Latino population there's like Latino administrators and counselors that maybe like, I could like feel more comfortable with. But at my school, it was kinda just like, not anybody that I could feel comfortable talking about that.

Like Belen, other young people in Georgia described not disclosing their status to high school guidance counselors or friends because they felt like they would not be able to help. Unfortunately, for many young people, this was true, but for Alondra, who was one of the few participants enrolled in college, a connection with a caring and knowledgeable teacher helped her navigate the college application process despite being undocumented. She reflected on his role in her life, a pivotal moment for her:

People talk about barriers to higher education and that glass-ceiling effect. I think people like him really help push people and not just in the big picture with motivation, but to have someone there to get you in through the nuts and bolts on how to do an application that you're unsure of. . . . In high school a lot of people become distant from their parents because it's that age where you want your independence and you're a little more frustrated; you want your space. Your parents aren't necessarily the go-to adults all the time—even if it's for something serious like college applications and talks about your legal status or anything like that. I think it's incredibly helpful to have . . . whether it's a teacher, or a mentor, some sort of adult to guide you and be there for support. Guidance counselors are also . . . technically I think it's a little bit of their job, but they're overwhelmed. I would say, in my case, it's not like the guidance counselor was completely unhelpful, but I definitely needed more information than she had.

Alondra's narrative reveals the complexity of the high school-to-college transition and the crucial role that institutional agents, such as guidance counselors, teachers, or school administrators, can play in facilitating or constraining this transition, particularly for first-generation students of color. As Alondra noted, her guidance counselor was not helpful as she planned to apply to college. Instead, a caring teacher both helped and motivated her.

Saul was also attending FU and, like many young people at FU, he had hopes of realizing his dreams of going to college. Saul was in the eleventh grade when Policies 4.1.6 and 4.3.4, collectively known as "the ban," took effect. During our interview, which we conducted at the dining table of his parents' home, he shared that it was during tenth grade that he became serious about attending college. He was looking forward to starting the college application process, but after learning that the ban would prevent him from attending, he fell into a depression. He stopped doing his homework and he let his grades slip. Despite this setback, in his senior year, with prodding from a good friend, Saul decided to explore community college as an option. He visited the admissions office of a local technical college, the closest two-year college, and learned the following:

> So, we went there and asked about the applications, and then that's when I found out again, they were like, "Well, these are the in-state tuition rates, but this is what you have to pay, out-of-state tuition, which is three or four times more," and I was like "wow, this is ridiculous" . . . I was like, "I'm not paying this, especially for a technical school."

Several of the undocumented youth I interviewed in Georgia echoed Saul's sentiment that the financial challenge of paying out-of-state tuition prevented them from attending even two-year colleges. For example, Georgia Perimeter College, a two-year college[1] in the Atlanta area, would cost an undocumented immigrant $21,000 for two years versus the $7,600 in-state tuition rate. Unlike California, where the in-state tuition policy AB540 facilitated access to two-year colleges for undocumented students even before the passage of the California Dream Act, the policy requiring undocumented immigrants to pay out-

---

1. In Georgia, the two-year college system includes both community colleges and technical colleges. Two-year colleges are run by both the University System of Georgia and the Technical College System of Georgia and are therefore subject to the out-of-state tuition policy set by the Georgia Board of Regents.

of-state tuition in Georgia meant that several college-aspiring undocumented young people were not continuing their formal education after high school.

Despite the significant financial challenges undocumented young people faced trying to attend college in Georgia, a handful were enrolled in college. At the time of our interview, Omar had been out of high school for two years and was one of four participants who were enrolled in or had attended college in the state. Omar attended a public university right out of high school, but he had to "stop out" because he could not afford it. He was taking a year off and planned to work and attend the two-year college in his community:

> It [his undocumented status] has, it has, because it's hard for me to pay for college. Last year, I attended [a state university], and it was hard because I was paying out-of-state tuition. I paid five grand for twelve credits . . . and here in [State Tech], I tried to apply earlier to enter spring semester. But apparently, their policies have changed, and now, even for Deferred Action students, from the beginning they're charging them as international. So that's three to four times . . .

As Omar emphasized, even attending a two-year college was out of his financial reach. Despite this, Omar was actively saving to return to college. He saved about $150 for college from each paycheck, but recently had been unable to save as much as he would have liked because his father, also an undocumented immigrant, was out of work. So, Omar contributed $100 to his family every week for food and bills, reducing the amount of money he could save so that he could return to the public university.

In addition to the requirement that undocumented immigrants pay out-of-state tuition. Another potentially consequential policy was enacted in January 2015 while I was doing my fieldwork. The Board of Regents announced that certain smaller colleges would merge with larger colleges to streamline administrative costs. Two of the colleges that were merging were Georgia Perimeter College, the two-year college in the Atlanta area, and Georgia State University, one of the three colleges included in the ban. The announcement created uncertainty about whether undocumented students would also be banned from Georgia Perimeter

College. Jovan, a twenty-three-year-old DACA recipient, was working at a Super Target and remarked that the merger created uncertainty for him and other students who might consider attending Georgia Perimeter:

> There is Georgia Perimeter, but um, it's soon merging with Georgia State University, and that's one of the schools where I'm banned from, so I don't know if they are going to continue the same policies of banning us from that. So, it's in a limbo altogether, and I don't really want to put up a fight with that.

The consolidation of several campuses across the state created a sense of anxiety about narrowing educational opportunities. While Policy 4.3.4 (out-of-state tuition) made the cost of attending two- and four-year colleges nearly impossible for undocumented young adults, Policy 4.1.6. (the ban from the top three colleges and universities) heightened the negative impact of seemingly neutral policies like consolidating smaller colleges and universities with larger ones. Participants asserted that, like most of their citizen classmates, they preferred to stay in the state of Georgia to attend college. This was due in part to their desire to be close to their parents, many of whom were also undocumented. Given these practical constraints, this meant that many of the undocumented young adults I interviewed were not enrolled in college, and with each passing year, their pathways to college were becoming more tenuous.

While the Board of Regents' policies presented structural barriers to college completion and entry for undocumented young adults, these policies also had symbolic implications. During our interviews, many undocumented young adults expressed feelings of rejection, disappointment, and frustration over these policies. Like Saul, who fell into a depression upon learning that his legal status would make it difficult for him to attend college, other undocumented young adults described similar instances of depression both during and after high school. Jovan, for example, recalled an incident at a party during his senior year of high school:

> I do remember this one time I went to a party, my friends and me were drinking, and you know, having fun, and I just broke down crying in front of them because I told them, you know, I couldn't go to school, you know, I couldn't do the military, I couldn't do all of this, and I felt just stuck.

For Jovan, who went to a predominantly white high school in a suburb of Atlanta, this party was one of the first times he revealed his legal status to his friends, who were not undocumented. While many of his friends planned to go to technical or state colleges, Jovan felt stuck and excluded from the opportunity to "go off and leave this small town to find something . . . figure out life." Both Araceli and her younger sister, who was also undocumented, worked hard in high school to take full advantage of the educational opportunities available to them, including taking advanced placement courses. Araceli, who described herself as a "very hard worker," also regularly worked fifty to sixty hours a week as a waitress at a local restaurant, both to contribute to her family's household income and to be able to save enough to eventually go to college. Because of her full-time work schedule, I interviewed her on her one day off during the week, and during our interview, she explained,

> It's just the limitation of what I can do frustrates me. It's frustrating. That's how I feel. I feel frustrated. I know for a fact that my parents do, too. They want us to go to school. They came here to give us a better life, to get a better education. The fact that I can't get it frustrates me. It makes me angry. I can't do anything about it. I don't have a say in the government. I can't vote. I can't. It's my country, too. This is all I know. The fact that they're limiting me to not only my potential, my success, my education, my right as a human being to get that education, frustrates me.

During our interview, it was clear that Araceli was proud of her work ethic and her contribution to her family's economic well-being. But like many of the undocumented young adults I interviewed in Georgia, she was frustrated that her intellect and her work ethic were not being used to improve her own and her family's lives. In short, Araceli and other undocumented youth felt that these restrictive policies not only set them up to fall short of reaching their own goals but also of the dreams their parents had when migrating to the United States.

While most of the young people I interviewed in Georgia aspired to attend four-year colleges, some had other educational dreams. Ines worked as a manager at a pizzeria. Her work schedule was demanding and unpredictable, and because of this, I interviewed her at the restaurant when her shift was over. Ines, who had done very well in high school, wanted to become a pastry chef. While she knew there were different routes she could take to achieve this, she wanted to attend a culinary arts program to give herself the best chance of securing a good job in a competitive industry. However, attending a culinary arts program at a two-year college or a culinary school was impossible because of the cost. During our interview, it became apparent that being prevented from attending school to become a pastry chef not only made her feel stuck but was also taking an emotional toll on Ines. Through tears, she told me, "I always get teary, because it means a lot to me. It means a lot to me to be able to go to school. I felt like, in a way, I felt like I had let my parents down, because I wasn't able to do more. But she [her mom] was like, 'You don't have to go to school to be good.'" Beyond being a loving response from a mother to her daughter, Ines' mom's comments reveal a deeper pressure that undocumented young people face, which is the idea that "good" immigrants, especially undocumented young people, continue their education beyond high school. "Good" immigrants honor their parents' migration sacrifices by going on to college, whether that is a two- or four-year university. While the Board of Regents policies created a structural barrier to upward mobility and had material consequences for young people's lives, their educational exclusion also had significant implications for their sense of belonging.

Legal Violence and the Educational Futures of Undocumented Young Adults

Immigration scholars Cecilia Menjivar and Leisy Abrego note that the ways that contemporary immigration laws are enacted and enforced constitute a form of legal violence, shaping and disrupting individual immigrants' lives on a routine basis. In both Los Angeles and Atlanta, the undocumented young people in this study faced blocked paths to mobility and, at times, intense stigmatization because of their racialized legal status. These blocked paths to mobility resulted in depression, lack of motivation, and altered expectations for the future. In Georgia, the transition out of high school is fraught with uncertainty and changing expectations. This experience mirrors that of Latinx undocumented young adults in California before the enactment of the AB 540 law and the California Dream Act, both of which made attending and paying for college easier (Abrego 2006). The two-pronged ban has both practical and symbolic implications for Latinx undocumented young adults in Georgia. The undocumented young adults I interviewed reported a range of academic performance indicators, from being enrolled in advanced placement courses to being on the regular track in their high schools. Regardless of their academic performance, they all expressed a desire to attend college, and eventually graduate from a four-year university. Despite this desire, many were not enrolled in college one, two, or three years after high school graduation. Many attributed this to the policy requiring that they pay out-of-state tuition at *any* public college or university. The Board of Regents Policy 4.3.4 (out-of-state tuition) has the greatest immediate impact on educational participation among undocumented young adults in Georgia. This educational exclusion not only has long-term implications for their structural incorporation but also has socioemotional implications, as Latinx undocumented young adults in Georgia must navigate the emotional ups and downs of feeling educationally untethered.

The Board of Regents Policy 4.1.6. (the ban from the top three public colleges) also had significant symbolic value for Latinx undocumented young adults in Georgia. I could not discern from the interviewees' self-reported academic experiences whether they were competitive candidates for the University of Georgia, Georgia State, or the Georgia Institute of Technology. Nevertheless, Latinx undocumented young adults in Georgia aspired to attend these institutions, both for the schools' reputation and their proximity to home. These aspirations, and their exclusion from these institutions, shaped their sense of belonging and perception of their future in the United States. As I recounted at the beginning of this chapter, Melanie and her twin sister's dream of attending the University of Georgia, a dream shared by many of the undocumented young adults I interviewed, was literally and figuratively shut down during the application process. This not only prevented them from applying to the University of Georgia but also sent them both into a period of depression and uncertainty. As Saul said during our interview, he felt like the State of Georgia no longer cared about what happened to him and his future after high school. During our interview, he expressed the belief that, through these two policies, the state was essentially saying to him,

"Okay, thanks for coming . . . good luck." While his statement was tinged with a bit of humor about the messages these policies send to undocumented young adults, there was an edge of bitterness to his sentiment that implied that he and other undocumented young adults living in Georgia felt unwanted and rejected by the place they considered home. Given the general political climate and attitudes toward undocumented immigrants in Georgia, this may indeed be the intent of these policies. Despite these policies, Latinx undocumented young adults are staying in the state and are, unfortunately, stagnating.

For Latinx undocumented young adults in California, their futures may seem more certain, but blocked opportunities manifest in different ways and at a later point in the transition to adulthood. While state laws and policies in California have alleviated much of the burden of attending public colleges in the state, undocumented young adults continue to face challenges. There are two key points in the educational pipeline for undocumented young adults in California. These include navigating the financial aid application process prior to entering college and then navigating a host of "college experiences" that are developed with citizen students in mind. This includes experiences such as getting an internship, studying abroad, living on campus, and being able to fully participate in the social life of colleges and universities. These key "college experiences" may have long-term implications for whether and how Latinx undocumented young adults are incorporating, both socioeconomically and socially.

Conclusion

In this chapter, I focused primarily on showing how state laws and policies shaped the educational pathways of Latinx undocumented young adults, a key dimension of their legal ecologies. As young people moved through high school, they began to experience the impacts of divergent higher education policies. State-level policies can ameliorate or exacerbate the exclusion of undocumented immigrants; however, because these state laws are nested within a broader federal context, the legal ecologies of Latinx undocumented adults in California and Georgia yielded similar feelings of exclusion at crucial points in their college-going journeys.

In both states, as high schoolers, undocumented youth embarked on their college choice journeys. For Latinx undocumented young people in the Los Angeles area, while there was apprehension about sharing their status with institutional agents in high school, a longstanding in-state tuition law (AB 540) coupled with the introduction of state and institutional financial aid (AB 130 and AB 131) created a more open policy context. While some young people in the Los Angeles area described counselors and teachers who were not as knowledgeable or supportive as they hoped, in general, college access laws facilitated their education. In stark contrast, the general political context in Georgia shut down young people's hopes and aspirations for attending college. Moving beyond the search phase of the college choice journey did not happen for many because of the exclusionary educational policies in the state (Board of Regents policies 4.1.6 and 4.3.4). The experiences of Latinx undocumented young adults in Georgia also highlight the crucial role that caring and knowledgeable teachers, counselors, or mentors can play, in part because, for most young people in the state, these institutional agents were missing from their college-going pursuits.

For high-achieving undocumented young adults in California and Georgia, the transition out of high school was also a contested period for negotiating feelings of belonging and membership, and ultimately, for both groups, altering expectations for one's future. For undocumented young people in both locales, a sense of belonging is a complex and layered experience. As education scholar Stephen Santa-Ramirez aptly notes, a sense of belonging is a difficult idea to define but it generally conveys the sense that "individuals feel welcomed, accepted and genuine members" of their respective communities (2022, 2). While undocumented young people in California were able to attend college and find some spaces of belonging, or a sense of belonging to their college campus community (Hurtado and Carter 1997; Santa-Ramirez 2022), the temporary nature of DACA made their long-term plans uncertain, impacting their overall sense of membership. In contrast, in Georgia, undocumented young people's exclusion from the formal higher education system directly impacted their overall sense of belonging even as FU created a microcontext of belonging. In both locales, undocumented young people had to create new orientations toward their futures with each passing year and as they navigated the shifting realities of their sociolegal contexts. As Menjivar and Abrego (2012) suggest, this process of altering expectations for one's future constitutes a distinct form of legal violence. In addition, the short-term security provided by DACA is tempered by the long-term uncertainty created by the absence of a pathway to citizenship. Nevertheless, there was a cautious optimism about DACA among participants. For example, undocumented young adults in both California and Georgia recognized the benefits of being able to move freely about the state without the fear of deportation. However, for some, DACA provided little to no opportunity to fulfill their larger goals and dreams. In this sense, the impact of state laws and policies on the futures of Latinx undocumented young adults in Georgia and California were more similar than I expected, revealing the overarching influence of a long-term solution via a pathway to citizenship.

CHAPTER 4

CITIZENSHIP, BELONGING, AND IDENTITY IN NEW AND OLD DESTINATIONS

On June 25, 2012, *Time* magazine featured journalist Jose Antonio Vargas on its cover. Vargas was born in the Philippines and migrated to the United States at the age of twelve to live with his grandparents in California. Like many undocumented young adults, Vargas learned he was in the United States without legal permission when he turned sixteen, and wanted to apply for a driver's license, a rite of passage for many young people. He disclosed his personal journey of navigating life as an undocumented young person in a June 2011 *New York Times* article entitled, "My Life as an Undocumented Immigrant." Vargas's disclosure of his status in such a public way came on the heels of a concerted effort by undocumented immigrant youth activists to "come out of the shadows" and advocate for a solution to the legal uncertainty undocumented young people face as they transition to and through adulthood. In fact, the *Time* magazine feature was published just days after President Barack Obama announced the Deferred Action for Childhood Arrivals (DACA) program in the Rose Garden of the White House.

On the *Time* magazine cover, Vargas is flanked by a sea of other undocumented immigrant young adults. In bold red letters across the top of the magazine cover is the statement "We are Americans,*" followed by "... *just not legally." The cover captured a narrative that has become prominent in the public discourse and some of the early scholarship about undocumented immigrant young adults; that they are American *but for* their legal status. The "aspiring American" narrative emerged in part as a strategy employed by advocates to appeal to a broader swath of potential supporters in the early 2000s when advocacy for the Development Relief and Education for Alien Minors (DREAM) Act was emerging (Monico 2020; Nicholls 2014). The DREAM Act, which was first introduced in 2001 and has been introduced several times since, would provide a pathway to citizenship for eligible undocumented immigrants. As the DREAM Act was introduced and re-introduced, the aspiring American narrative became synonymous with the quintessential "dreamer," or a high-achieving, otherwise law-abiding, young person who came to the United States through no fault of their own (Abrego and Negrón-Gonzales 2020; Monico 2020). These narratives are often used interchangeably by the media; political allies, for example, legislators and citizen educators; and some undocumented youth activists, to make claims to membership in the American polity. While the "aspiring American" and "dreamer" frames capture important aspects of the predicament of undocumented immigrant youth, namely that they have spent most of their lives in the United States, have been influenced by American culture, and yet have no claim to formal citizenship; these narratives flatten the varied and rich lived experience of undocumented immigrant youth. Furthermore, this framing rests largely on notions of deservingness that exclude a significant portion of undocumented immigrant youth (Dingeman-Cerda et al. 2017). As undocumented immigrant young people themselves took more ownership of the movement and its message, a critique emerged of the aspiring American and dreamer narratives. This critique was based on an inherent understanding of the exclusionary dimensions of these narratives. It also reflected an understanding that "Americanness" is racialized and has long excluded people of color, including Latinxs in the United States, from the full benefits of citizenship (Flores-Gonzalez 2017).

In this chapter, I explore the intersections of race and legal status to highlight how Latinx undocumented young adults articulate what it meant to them to be American. The experiences of the undocumented young adults I interviewed reveal a nuanced relationship with notions of citizenship, belonging, and ethnic identity—one that is more complex than the simple characterization of these young people as aspiring Americans. Undocumented young people's legal ecologies influenced how they articulated a sense of belonging by claiming but also rejecting facets of this "American" narrative. As I discussed in the previous chapter, Latinx undocumented youth navigate a sociolegal context that creates simultaneous inclusion and exclusion, particularly as they transition out of high school and into early adulthood. Undocumented young people's sense of belonging is deeply intertwined with their socialization experiences in school. Inclusion in the K–12 system not only inculcated undocumented young people with American beliefs, values, and norms but also contributed to a sense of belonging. As their educational belonging is disrupted either through exclusion from college access, as is the case in Georgia, or through incomplete inclusion in college experiences, as is the case in California, their sense of belonging is also disrupted. While DACA shields eligible undocumented immigrant youth from deportation, they remain exposed to a broader public discourse that paints Latinx undocumented immigrants as a threat and a target for deportation (Chavez 2008). Undocumented young adults' progressive exclusion from social institutions and social life as they age significantly shapes their personal experiences of illegality and their experiences of what it means to be Americans (Gonzales 2016).

As I discussed in chapter 2, these young people's understandings of illegality developed long before they transitioned out of the legally protected space of schools. Undocumented young adults in both California and Georgia described shared experiences of discrimination experienced by their parents and family members that, in conjunction with their own social exclusion in early adulthood, shaped their ambivalence about being "American." Their ambivalence reflects a process of making sense of the concrete benefits of formal legal citizenship, or legally becoming American, and their experiences of social inclusion and legal exclusion. To fully understand the patterns that emerge from interviews, it is important to understand the relationships between citizenship, belonging, and ethnic identity.

Citizenship, Belonging, and Intersectional Identities

According to Nira Yuval-Davis (2006), "identities are narratives, or stories that people tell about who they are (and who they are not)" (202). These narratives reflect the groups and spaces to which we feel we belong and those to which we do not. For undocumented immigrant youth, their narrative, or identity, is informed by an experience of membership that is at once exclusive and inclusive (Glenn 2011; Gonzales 2016). Inherent in this paradox is the tension between formal citizenship and substantive citizenship. While undocumented immigrant youth and undocumented members of their families are denied legal recognition, membership is not defined *only* by law. Formal citizenship, in the form of legal permission to be in the United States, is often at odds with the inclusion of undocumented immigrant youth in at least one key social institution: public schools. Research about the experiences of undocumented immigrant youth is situated at this (dis)juncture and reveals the paradox of this experience (Abrego 2008; Cebulko 2014; Gleeson and Gonzales 2012; Gonzales 2016). These studies document the acute personal sense of exclusion that undocumented immigrant youth experience as they transition out of high school and into more uncertain futures.

Undocumented immigrant youth also make this transition during a key stage in their lives and, therefore, in the identity development process. During the period of late adolescence through early adulthood, young people, regardless of their legal status, are asking, "Who am I?" and "What will I be?" (Jones and Abes 2013). In the sociological tradition, who we are, or what is referred to as "the self," develops out of interaction with the social world and structures, including systems of privilege and oppression. For undocumented young adults, a critical structure is their legal status, a social and historical construction that intersects with racial and ethnic identity. As sociologists Elizabeth Aranda, Elizabeth Vaquera, and Isabel Sousa-Rodriguez (2015) argue, the identity development process for undocumented youth is shaped by the personal and cultural trauma of being members of both marginalized racial groups *and* a group that is legally excluded, requiring an understanding of the interrelated and interdependent nature of these experiences.

As Aranda and colleagues aptly note, for undocumented immigrant young adults, their experience of personal trauma happens as they begin to transition to adulthood. In the case of the undocumented young adults who were transitioning to adulthood in the Atlanta area, being excluded from the top three institutions in the state, even as many were academically eligible to attend, is an example of personal trauma. Although in the Los Angeles area, undocumented young adults were able to go to college, as they navigated the pathway through the college, they also experienced personal trauma through incomplete belonging or exclusion from educational experiences and opportunities afforded to their citizen peers—for example, changing career trajectories based on their legal status or facing challenges paying for college even with institutional aid. In both states, uncertainty about their long-term futures creates a sense of both present and anticipatory trauma for these young adults. The cultural and collective trauma of anti-immigrant rhetoric and the vulnerability their parents faced navigating daily life also shaped the way that undocumented young adults in both regions felt about "being American." Yet, "feeling American" is an important measure of immigrant integration, as this is a crucial dimension of belonging.

Research into the incorporation experiences of immigrant children specifically examines ethnic identity development as a sign of how immigrant youth are assimilating, or not assimilating, into the United States (Feliciano 2009; Portes and Rumbaut 2001). Identificational assimilation (Gordon 1964) is the culmination of the assimilation process marked by self-identification as only American. However, as Portes and Rumbaut (2001) note, identificational assimilation is not available to racialized immigrants who experience prejudice and discrimination in the United States. Instead, they suggest that four patterns of ethnic self-identification emerge, with "American" being only one option, and including (1) national origin identity, (2) hyphenated identity, (3) American identity, and (4) a panethnic identity (Rumbaut 1994). These patterns of ethnic self-identification provide a helpful starting point for understanding how racialized young people may choose to identify ethnically. Yet, ethnic identity, like other identities, is both dynamic and contextual. For Latinx undocumented young adults, in addition to being racialized immigrants, they also experience legal exclusion, which may impact their ethnic identity development process differently than their U.S.-born, second-generation counterparts.

Scholars find that patterns of ethnic identity develop in response to contexts and experiences over the life course (Feliciano 2009; Portes and Rumbaut 2001; Phinney 1993). As I discussed earlier, the transition from adolescence to young adulthood is a crucial period in the ethnic identity development process (Jones and Abes 2013; Phinney 1993). For many Latinx undocumented young adults, this period coincides with the transition out of the legally protected space of the K–12 school system and into a period of "learning to be illegal" (Gonzales 2016). These direct experiences of legal exclusion, including difficulty navigating milestones in the transition to adulthood, may influence Latinx undocumented young adults' sense of belonging and their ethnic identity. As undocumented youth begin to feel the direct effects of their undocumented status, the potential for experiences of discrimination may also increase; as previous research suggests, direct experiences of discrimination can thicken ethnic identity (Portes and Rumbaut 2001). In addition to personal experiences of discrimination, hostile political contexts can also strengthen ethnic identity and lead individuals to develop a *reactive ethnicity*. Reactive ethnicities emerge in response to "perceived threats, discrimination, persecution, and exclusion" (Rumbaut 2008, 110). Tovar and Feliciano (2009) find, for example, that the Sensenbrenner Bill, an especially punitive anti-immigrant bill proposed in 2005, heightened Mexican American college students' self-identification as Mexican.

In the past thirty years, the national climate has become particularly hostile toward Latinx undocumented immigrants, with scholars describing current conditions enacting legal violence on undocumented immigrants (DeGenova 2002; Menjivar and Abrego 2012). This hostile sociopolitical context intersected with racialized notions of "Americanness" to create nuanced and often complicated ideas about citizenship, national and ethnic identity, and belonging for Latinx undocumented young adults. The aspiring American narrative—along with other key factors including state laws and policies, experiences of discrimination, and the presence or absence of other Latinxs—influenced the complex relationship Latinx undocumented young adults developed in relation to Americanness and, importantly, their sense of belonging. This complexity was reflected in the tension between the narrative of Americanness that is rooted in the experiences of undocumented immigrant youth who have lived most of their lives in the United States, and the reality that "Americanness" has long excluded certain groups from full participation as citizens.

Notions of citizenship and Americanness have historically been racialized as white in the United States, excluding members "whose ethnic, racial, or religious backgrounds highlight their cultural differences and limit their access to the rights and privileges of citizenship," or citizens who do not belong (Flores-Gonzales 2017, 10; Castles and Davidson 2000). For the undocumented young people in this book, their ethnic and racial identity, coupled with the reality that they are members of the undocumented 1.5 generation, created conflict around their sense of identity, specifically their national identity, or Americanness. As Nilda Flores-Gonzales finds in her expansive study of Latinx millennials, this friction reflects the racial and cultural dimensions that comprise ethnoracial citizenship, or "how Latinos are defined as outsiders of the national community and how they deploy counternarratives to stake claims of belonging" (2017, 154).

In this chapter, I examine how the legal ecologies of undocumented young adults shaped nuanced ideas about the value of formal legal citizenship, their ideas about what it means to be American, and their connections to their ethnic identity. As discussed earlier in this book, young people who grew up in Los Angeles described a less overtly hostile climate than respondents in the Atlanta area. This shaped their perceptions in early adulthood of the relationship between place and belonging, which was complicated by the multilayered nature of place, which included where they grew up and lived *and* the United States more broadly. I employ an approach that acknowledges the relationship between legal status and racialization. While the prevalence of the Latinx threat narrative was prominent in the Nuevo South, it also had a national presence (Browne and Odem 2012; Marrow 2011). In an increasingly hostile and threatening political climate, undocumented youths' claims to an American identity directly challenged racist nativism that frames undocumented immigrants in dehumanizing ways. I examine young people's descriptions of experiences of discrimination within these different contexts—discrimination being, again, a key factor in shaping ethnic identity. Finally, I discuss how Latinx undocumented young adults in Los Angeles and Atlanta articulated their ethnoracial and national identities in response to the simultaneous inclusion and exclusion that they experienced as a result of living in a racialized society like the United States.

Ambivalent Americans: Undocumented Young Adults and Identity in Los Angeles and Atlanta

Despite very different political contexts and differing experiences of discrimination, rather than a strong pattern of ethnic identification emerging *between* state contexts, a pattern of ethnic identification *across* state

contexts emerged. While political context and experiences of discrimination were salient in shaping Latinx undocumented young adults' ethnic
identification later in life, undocumented young adults in both Los Angeles and Atlanta described a complex relationship with Americanness
and their own ethnic identity. This finding is surprising but not entirely
unexpected; it speaks to the enduring power of the uncertainty created
by federal law in shaping how Latinx undocumented young adults experience belonging. While undocumented young people clearly understood
that they were outside the category of formal legal citizenship, their experiences of substantive citizenship or social inclusion were deeply at odds
with their legal exclusion. The conflation of citizenship, Americanness,
and whiteness profoundly shaped how they saw themselves fitting in,
or not fitting in, with the imagined community of America (Anderson
2016). In the following sections, I examine some of the prominent patterns of ethnic identification that emerged among young people. I start
by discussing how Latinx undocumented young adults in both regions
conceptualize what it means to be American, which, unsurprisingly, they
primarily associated with whiteness. However, they also distinguished
themselves from U.S.-born Latinxs, revealing how their ethnoracial identity and legal status intersected. Finally, I discuss how Latinx undocumented young adults conceptualized the benefits of DACA and potential
citizenship, which they approached with a sense of ambivalence or a set
of feelings that were at times contradictory.

The Contradictions of Being Labeled American for Undocumented Young Adults

The interviews I conducted with young people covered a range of topics
but focused on several outcomes and experiences, including identity. In
one portion of the interview, we talk about their experiences and ideas
about what it means to be an American or a citizen. While their experiences and understandings of immigration law are woven throughout
their interview narratives, this specific series of questions often elicits
a physical response—respondents may laugh, shrug their shoulders, or
sigh. These physical responses and their subsequent reflections about
what it means to be a citizen, to belong, or to be an American, are indica-
tive of the lived contradictions they encounter daily. While I have a hunch

that ideas about belonging and exclusion cross their mind daily, they are likely passing thoughts as these young people move from school to work, work to home, and home to hanging out with friends, partners, and family. This series of questions in our interviews offers undocumented young adults a chance to reflect and articulate their everyday experiences of belonging and exclusion, and what it means to them to be an American.

The most common verbal response to questions about citizenship, belonging, and what it means to be American was some variation of "I am having a hard time with this question." While my interviews were open-ended, this series of questions often took the following form: "What does it mean to you to be an American? What does it mean to you to be a citizen? What does citizenship mean to you? How do you identify?" To make sense of young people's responses, Nilda Flores-Gonzales's (2017) research about Latinxs, race, and belonging is especially relevant here as she identifies the cultural and racial dimensions of American national identity that exclude Latinxs from the national imagination. For the Latinx millennials in her study, Americanness was synonymous with whites of European descent (a racial category), and cultural practices or tropes that defined what it meant to be American. Flores-Gonzales asserts that, because of their racial identity and cultural practices, Latinx millennials are outside the construct of ethnoracial citizenship, leaving them to develop and define counternarratives of what it means to be American and, in this way, assert belonging.

Julieta, who was twenty-three at the time of our interview, migrated to Los Angeles from El Salvador when she was seven years old. When her mother migrated to the United States, Julieta stayed behind and lived in El Salvador with her grandmother. When her mother sent for her, the time she had spent in El Salvador with her grandmother had created a stronger tie to her home country. However, her sixteen years living in the United States had also made her feel like she was American. At the time of our interview, she had just graduated from college and was preparing to attend graduate school. In response to my question "What does it mean to you to belong in America? Do you feel like you belong?" she answered,

> The reason why I'm having a hard time with this question is because . . . I thought I want to be American, and I am an American. I love this country,

but once I started gaining a critical aspect of this country, it's not so much that I don't want to be American, it's that I want to keep in mind my roots, keep in mind where I came from, and at the same time contribute to this society. . . . I want to say words in Spanish and be able to express myself and express my culture, and if that's not considered American, because American is mostly associated with white, Eurocentric kind of thing . . . so I'm kind of in limbo because I don't feel completely American in the mainstream term of white [laughs].

Julieta's answer reveals her understanding of the racial dimensions of national identity, and racialization of American identity as a white, Eurocentric identity. Rather than draw from American tropes, Julieta instead emphasizes her desire to stay connected to her Salvadoran roots, her language—Spanish—and her culture. It is these experiences that she suggests may ultimately exclude her from "mainstream" Americanness. At the same time, she asserts her identity as an American and her desire to be recognized as American, not by assimilating but by integrating the culture and language of El Salvador with her experiences growing up in the United States. Further complicating her thoughts about being American was her growing understanding of the ways the United States excluded people of color and immigrants.

Like Julieta, Latinx undocumented young adults, regardless of where they grew up, were cognitively and emotionally assimilating long-held desires to be seen as American, a growing understanding of the exclusionary and racialized nature of that category, and a complicated relationship with their home countries. José, who lived in the greater Los Angeles area, stated,

"I've never really considered myself an 'American-American.' I kind of don't like the idea of being an 'American-American.'" I asked José what that meant. He responded, "Going to baseball games, going to football games, driving the sedan. I guess I really—I don't want to say it, but I'll say it—a whitewashed culture. I'm like, I can't fathom the idea that I'd do that, you know?"

José associated being American with specific cultural behaviors that he rejected because he associated these tropes with being whitewashed, a form of assimilation that included a rejection of his Mexican culture. Later in our interview, he admitted that, while he could never imagine himself "assimilating" by assuming these behaviors, he also could not imagine living in Mexico. José's mother, who had returned to Mexico and was living there, gave him a firsthand sense of life in Mexico, and he remarked: "I don't think I can go back there, even if for a short vacation . . . so, we've been here most of our lives. We know a lot of stuff, you know?" José's and Julieta's reticence to embrace the term "American" as a core identity reflected the complicated relationship that Latinx undocumented young people had with Americanness and the reality that they were American in many ways by virtue of growing up in the United States.

Young people from the Atlanta area expressed similar feelings of being different. Melanie, who migrated to the Atlanta area from Mexico at the age of two, echoed Julieta's sense of not quite belonging in the United States but conversely could not imagine truly belonging in her home country. As we discussed her experiences growing up in the Atlanta area at the kitchen table in her parent's home, she explained,

> It's just like growing up, like it's weird, because growing up in a culture, like you didn't feel American; obviously you're very different. But it's also a lot different than, like, Mexican people growing up here as citizens because they don't have to deal with that loss. So, it's like I always felt like I was in between, I guess. In between being Mexican and American.

Like Julieta and José, Melanie, who grew up in a predominantly white suburb of Atlanta, expressed a feeling of *ni de aquí, y ni de allá* (neither from here, neither from there). While Melanie does not quite articulate what it means to be American as sharply as Julieta did, she does distinguish herself, a Mexican undocumented immigrant, from American culture. She also describes leaving Mexico as "having to deal with a loss," something that she states distinguishes her experience, and those of other immigrant youth, from U.S.-born Mexicans who have a claim to legal citizenship, highlighting the salience of legal status. This sense of loss was shaped by the reality that, like many participants, she had never been able to return to their country of origin. DACA was relatively new, and Advance Parole, or the opportunity to temporarily travel outside the United States for humanitarian, employment, or educational reasons, had not yet been introduced (Immigrant Legal Resource Center 2022). At the time of the interviews, undocumented young people were unsure when they might be able to return to their countries of origin. Even if they migrated at a young age and had little to no memory of their time in their home country, there was a deep sense of loss.

Distinct from U.S.-born Latinxs, undocumented young people's feelings about Americanness were shaped not only by ethnoracial citizenship, or race and culture, but also by their legal status. I met Marco for our interview at a café in Downtown Atlanta, and he was one of the few young people enrolled in college in the state. He migrated to Atlanta with his mom when he was seven years old to meet his dad, who had migrated earlier that same year. During high school, Marco distinguished himself academically and secured a scholarship to a public university in southern Georgia, a place I sensed was not his top choice or a path he would have chosen but for his legal status. He shared,

> My senior year, I was able to get a scholarship and along with a private scholarship to pay for my first year in college [at State University], and I've been there ever since. I can't go to the top-five universities. So, I have to go to the not-top-five universities. Then I have to [have] $13,000, so it's really hard for someone who is undocumented to afford college.

As we talked about his experiences growing up in Atlanta, his participation in activism, and his goal of becoming a journalist, he shared that it was not until 2011 that he began to feel the stigma of being undocumented, as he recounted, "It was in 2011 when Georgia passed the ban of undocumented students from the top-five universities. . . . And it was only when these policies were put in place that I began to feel threatened." While Marco was one of the few undocumented young people I interviewed enrolled in college in Georgia, the sense that despite focusing on getting good grades in high school, he was pushed to attend a non-top-five university shaped his rejection of an American identity, even as he felt like his experiences reflected the American dream. He shared,

> I stopped romanticizing being an American and assimilating. I became more resentful. As you grow more, you read more, and you become aware of things, and I just gave up on the idea of being an American, and I also gave up on the idea of being a Mexican. . . . I just want to call myself undocumented. My perspective of politics is seeing how much I have been

treated and realizing that, if I were a common American, I would have the privileges of an American even if I wasn't born here. . . . You don't see Americans . . . you don't see general students showing up to rallies too because the ban doesn't affect them as documented people. So, you can't claim a title and be treated in an opposite manner.

As Marco so adeptly observes, if he were truly seen as an American, he would be able to pursue whatever educational path he wanted, whether at a top-five college in Georgia or elsewhere. His comment also reflects the dialogic nature of national identity—that is, he can claim American-ness, but being subject to exclusionary policies firmly places him on the outside of that national identity. For Marco and other undocumented young people, their legal status combined with their ethnoracial identity amplified their place outside of the national imagination. The intersection of these identities shaped their ideas about who is, and what it means to be, American. Latinx undocumented young people identified both racial and cultural dimensions of national identity while also highlighting the material implications of their legal status for their sense of Americanness. Regardless of the age at which they migrated to the United States and whether their families settled in the Los Angeles or Atlanta area, respondents described a sense of connection to and, therefore, a sense of loss of, the country they were born in. This experience of being between two countries was prevalent in the narratives of the Latinx undocumented young adults interviewed in both Los Angeles and Atlanta.

Reactive Ethnicities: The Complications of Identifying Your "Home Country"

Latinx undocumented young adults in Los Angeles and Atlanta who identified both with their country of origin *and* as Americans were wrestling with making sense of their seemingly contradictory attachments to their home country and the United States. Jasmin, who migrated to the Atlanta area when she was three years old and had lived in the United States for fifteen years, discussed a photography project she had just completed as part of a class for Freedom University (FU). Her subject was her brother, who was a couple of years older than her and a DACA recipient. She composed the photograph to represent an identity crisis:

> I had an identity crisis for the longest . . . I remember we had a photog-
> raphy class last semester. I used my brother as the subject. I, like, got a
> paper bag and put it over his head with a question mark, and I picked up
> the American flag on one side and the Mexican flag on the other side. . . .
> I didn't know where I was from because all my life I have been here. But
> you're not supposed to be here, you're not American. So, I was like, I'm
> not American, but I wasn't Mexican, because I don't know barely any of
> the culture or the slang.

For Jasmin, her self-described identity crisis was rooted in her experience
of growing up in the United States but with the knowledge that she did
not have legal permission to be here or was not supposed to be here.
Like Marco, her legal status, and not her ethnic identity as a Mexican,
precluded her from "being American." Yet, she also did not feel like she
was Mexican because she had not been immersed in that culture enough
to understand shared practices like slang. At the time of our interview,
though, she was becoming more comfortable with claiming an American identity. Both Jasmin and her brother were regular students at FU,
and she and others learned about the complicated history of race in the
United States and how even those with citizenship, like African Americans, had long been excluded from full inclusion in the American polity.
Jasmin and other students who attended Freedom University understood
how claiming an American identity, especially in a hostile state like Georgia, was empowering. Given that her own sense of Mexican identity was
tenuous because she had grown up in the United States, she also seemed
to struggle with whether embracing an American identity meant a rejection of her Mexican identity. Nevertheless, as she described, this greater
sense of peace with being American influenced her decision to include
the American flag alongside the Mexican flag in the photo, an image that
she felt was representative of her personal journey.

Undocumented young adults from both states expressed concern that,
although they felt they were American in their tastes and their childhood
experiences, solely claiming an American identity could be construed as
denying their country of origin. Nallely, who migrated from El Salvador
to an hour outside of Atlanta and had lived in the United States for fourteen years, asserted that while she considered herself American, she was
not denying her "culture." She elaborated:

I don't think that, by considering myself an American, I'm denying my El Salvadoran identity. Some people are very like, "It's one or the other." You have to recognize the possibility that both exist. At this point when you live longer in another country, it's been your native country, it's hard not to consider yourself an American from that aspect.

During our interviews, Latinx undocumented young adults from Los Angeles and Atlanta expressed a sense that identifying as only "American" would constitute making a choice or signaling assimilation. So, identifying with their country of origin (El Salvador in Nallely's case) and identifying as American helped Latinx undocumented young adults integrate their bicultural experiences and reflect their reality as members of the 1.5 generation. As Nallely clearly states, by the time of our interview, she had lived longer in the United States than in El Salvador. As she notes, she considers America her native country, a reflection of not only the length of time she had lived in the United States but also of having spent formative years in another country, not El Salvador. Manuel, who initially migrated with his family to California and then eventually moved with them to Atlanta, explained, "We love Mexico, we say we're Mexicans, but we're from the United States. . . . I do consider myself an American. Even though I'm Mexican, I'm a Mexican-American. . . . I consider the United States my country, too."

Like Manuel, Miriam, who grew up in Los Angeles, came to a hyphenated identity, but after a long personal journey of making peace with the United States. At the time of our interview, she had not completely gotten over her the sense that, when she was growing up, the United States was tearing her family part, and "that I couldn't see the people I used to see before and I couldn't leave when I wanted to leave; it made me irritated and very mad. As I started growing up, I realized all the things I couldn't do." Miriam had developed a deep animosity toward the United States, which pushed her toward a Mexican identity. In conjunction with her father instilling a sense of pride about being from Mexico, this further shaped her ethnic identity.

So I identify as Mexican because I always had that resentment of leaving Mexico and always that nostalgia of how it would be to live there. I am proud to be from there, so I do identify as Mexican because of that. For

Chicana, I think that one is more because of what I'm doing now. Before, I used to have this idea that I'm Mexican and that's it, but I think that lately, because I've been working as part of an undocumented student organization at the university, I kind of started realizing more of how much I didn't hate the U.S. I don't hate it as I thought I did before. I appreciate what I've done here and the things I can do because of it. That's why I identify as Chicana, because I am from here. A part of me, regardless of whether I was born here or not, I lived here all my life.

Interestingly enough, it was Miriam's involvement in the undocumented student organization on her college campus that guided her to identify as Chicana—a politicized Mexican American identity. Although Miriam never mentioned identifying as American, acknowledging that she was from "here," that is, the United States, constituted a step toward a hyphenated, albeit politicized identity.

For Latinx undocumented young adults who identified as solely from their home country, their choices revealed an equally complex relationship to ideas of home, growing up in the United States, and Americanness. While we might expect Latinx undocumented young adults from Atlanta to develop the *strongest* sense of connection to their home countries because of the hostile climate, respondents from both Los Angeles and Atlanta ethnically self-identified as being from their country of origin. Luz conveyed her understanding of her ethnic identity in one of the more interesting ways that came up during interviews:

I'm not an American, I'm not. I guess I have . . . what's it called? Assimilated to it. I do listen to music and all that stuff, and I have a couple white friends, and I am in higher education, which is not common among Latinos, but I'm not an American. If you were to ask me, Mexico and U.S. get into a war, who would you support? Mexico. . . . It's because I feel like America isn't really what I thought it would be. . . . America is so selfish, it's so politics, it's all money. I do believe that's what America stands for, not Americans, but America.

Although Luz grew up in California, in a relatively welcoming state policy context, and was enrolled in a four-year university from which she was about to graduate, she was reluctant to identify as American because of her ideas about what the country stood for. Luz's comments reveal the complicated nature of identifying and distinguishing the cultural practices and values she associated with being American. As she shared, in some ways, she believes she has assimilated, listening to American music and having a "couple white friends." Yet, she distinguishes these signals of cultural assimilation from values that are associated with America as an institution and, as she noted, not the people themselves. She conceptualized her ethnic identity choice as a hypothetical war. Her choice, "not American," was focused on rejecting negative values that she perceived as American values. Like Luz, Aurora, who migrated when she was eleven years old, also identified as only Mexican. Earlier, she described a belief that her hometown in the Los Angeles area was not that different from where she lived in Mexico, and her ethnic identity choice was motivated by a sense of pride.

> I'm really proud to be Mexican. I'm always talking Spanish when I can. It just makes me feel more like home. I don't know, it just feels good to be Mexican. I respect America because thanks to it I learned English, I have a great education, and hopefully I can get a good job. I have no regrets towards it. I just don't like the people that are so negative and have negative thoughts towards immigrants. I don't know. I don't know if I see myself as an American.

Despite growing up in a community where she felt particularly safe and describing generally positive experiences in her predominantly Latinx high school, Aurora's ethnic identity was tied to pride. Yet, like Luz, it was *also* connected to a rejection of a perceived value held by some Americans, in this case, anti-immigrant sentiment. Reflecting the two-way nature of national identity—that is, claiming inclusion and being included—as an immigrant herself, she could not fully embrace an American identity, which for her was tied to negative perceptions about immigrants, highlighting how contextual factors like sociolegal context can shape identity.

Ines described her experience of a changing Atlanta. When she first arrived in the area, she remarked that her mother would make tortillas from scratch because there were no Hispanic stores that sold tortillas. However, she and I conducted the interview at a pizza place tucked away in a Latinx shopping market that included a *taquería*, *carnicería*, and *panadería*. Despite the shift in the Latinx population, during our interview, Ines described the current context in Georgia as especially racist toward undocumented Latinx immigrants. She listed several instances when either her father or her uncles were harassed while driving. She also recounted that, when she accompanied her brother, who was born in the United States, to apply for his driver's license, he was questioned by the DMV clerk about whether his birth certificate was real. She described her brother as looking "Hispanic . . . and so he doesn't look like he was born here." These experiences shaped her ethnic identity, and during our interview, she stated,

> I always say I'm from Mexico. I don't like to say that I'm from here, because I don't know, I just . . . I always think about that. I always say I'm from Mexico. I don't know much about it [Mexico]. It's kind of embarrassing sometimes . . . but I always say I'm from Mexico. Even my brother says he's from Mexico.

For Ines and her brother, a U.S.-born citizen, their experiences of discrimination, seen both through their parents' eyes and their own, strengthened their ethnic identity, demonstrating how the racial politics of visibility impacts Latinx young people regardless of their legal status (Flores-Gonzales 2017) Annette, who migrated from Peru and lived about an hour outside of Atlanta, stated that she was proud of her Peruvian heritage, although she realized that she grew up as "American."

> I am very strong to my roots and if they ask me if I rather be an American or Peruvian, I am going to choose Peruvian because that is who I am. I am from Peru 100 percent. My family is like an American, that is how I grew up, that is how I was raised, as an American. But who I am as a person, I am a Peruvian and I am proud of it.

Annette discussed her ethnic identity in terms of a choice or seemingly being forced to choose an identity, and this is reflective of the choices that Latinx undocumented young adults must make when it comes to their ethnic identity. While it is well-established that ethnic identities are shifting and contextual, I expected Latinx undocumented young adults to be more certain about the benefits, both perceived and actual, of citizenship. On the contrary, as I learned, Latinx undocumented young adults in both Los Angeles and Atlanta were ambivalent about citizenship.

Latinx Undocumented Young Adults Questioning Citizenship

As music in Spanish blared over a loudspeaker in a café in Santa Ana, California, I interviewed Karina, who migrated to Orange County with her parents and her brother. Both she and her brother applied and received DACA, which has allowed Karina to work in the field she trained in during college, child development. At the time of our interview, she had graduated from a California State University in the area and was on her second postcollege job. She also recently purchased a brand-new car, of which she was very proud, and she was considering moving out of her parents' mobile home. Karina attributed much of her success to the passage of DACA, but even with this, she remained ambivalent or even hostile to the idea of becoming a citizen. During our interview, she explained:

> It's just very frustrating. I think the only reason to become a U.S. citizen is for the benefits it would come with, not to identify as "Oh, now I'm a U.S. citizen. Have more respect for me. . . ." I think the benefits would be a reason for me to become, if it was possible, but I've come to a place where I don't *desire* to be a U.S. citizen.

Karina's ambivalence about being an American may have been rooted in her experiences as an undocumented student activist and Chicanx Studies major in college. Like Karina, during the process of "learning to be illegal" (Gonzales 2011), other respondents went through periods of wanting to be a citizen, primarily for the practical benefits it offered. As Brenda, who grew up in Los Angeles and had DACA, elaborated, "This might differ with me, but if I get my papers or not . . . I don't know what I would do if I had them. Does that make sense? Because I'm used to not being with them." Brenda's reflection highlights the enduring power of growing up undocumented. Like Brenda, Carlos grew up in the Los Angeles area and had DACA. He shared her ambivalence about the possibility of becoming a citizen. I asked him: "If you had the option to become a citizen, is that something you would do?" He responded: "I don't know. That's always been, for me, a complicated question, I think because being undocumented becomes part of your identity, so it's really complex to think of yourself as anything different. Obviously, there is a slew of legal benefits that come along with it; that's definitely great." Even though Brenda and Carlos, like most of the participants, had DACA, they expressed feelings of ambivalence about the possible impact of citizenship on their sense of belonging and identity. When undocumented young adults in both Los Angeles and Atlanta discussed citizenship, they were most enthusiastic about the opportunity to travel—specifically, to travel to their home countries. Ariana lived in Atlanta and had an adventurous spirit that came through during our interview, commented: "I mean honestly, I really don't care if I'm a citizen or not, the only reason I would want it is because I love traveling. Without it, you can't do it." Besides the opportunity to travel that citizenship would open up, Latinx undocumented young adults expressed an understanding that if they could qualify for citizenship, they might be able to apply for their undocumented parents, an opportunity that some were waiting for younger, U.S.-born siblings to act upon. But their reasons for desiring citizenship were pragmatic. Very few expressed what Jennifer expressed toward the end of her interview when I asked if, given the opportunity to become a U.S. citizen, she would become one, she replied: "Yeah, no doubt." Asked what this would mean for her, she explained:

> I really feel like I'm from here. No matter, even though I'm undocumented, this is where I'm from. If I were to go back to Mexico, I would feel like I am visiting, not like it's where I'm from. It [being a citizen] would just be kind of like being accepted into a place where you already feel you belong.

For Jennifer, having citizenship would be a formal acknowledgment of a feeling she already has, that of belonging. For Jennifer, acceptance and legal citizenship were inseparable. But for most Latinx undocumented young adults, citizenship was just a pragmatic step to securing a future for themselves and their families.

Conclusion

While Latinx undocumented young adults in Los Angeles and Atlanta described distinct social contexts and experiences of discrimination, their ethnic identities did not follow a clear between-state pattern, revealing the long reach of the federal immigration context in shaping these young adults' ideas about ethnoracial identity and citizenship. Particularly hostile contexts can strengthen immigrant youth's ties to their home countries, and Latinx undocumented young adults who identify more strongly with their country of origin (e.g., Mexico, Peru) may be reacting to an increasingly anti-immigrant context at the national level. Inaction at the federal level has opened the door to hostile policies at the state level and discrimination. While Latinx undocumented young adults in both California and Georgia expressed gratitude for the opportunities that living in the United States afforded them, they hesitated to embrace an American identity, demonstrating their understanding that Americanness has long excluded people of color and immigrants (Flores-Gonzales 2017).

For Latinx undocumented young adults in both states who identified as either a hyphenated identity or as being from their country of origin and being American, this reflected a process of integrating what can seem at times to be two contradictory identities. These undocumented young adults often expressed a sense that to choose one or the other was a false choice and not representative of their identity experiences. While one could assume that choosing both identities signals an alignment with the "dreamer" narrative of Americanness, the tension and hesitation that was conveyed during interviews signals a dialogical process between feelings of Americanness and pride in one's cultural heritage. For some Latinx undocumented young adults, claiming the identity of "American" and their country of origin was a strategy for empowerment. This may be where the social movement narrative of "Americanness" is rooted, but in many ways, that message has been misconstrued as patriotic discourse or loyalty. So, the tension I sensed in interviews when I asked Latinx undocumented young adults if they "considered themselves American" reflected a vision for America that included them and their families. Even those who chose their country of origin as their primary ethnic identity did so in conversation with perceptions of the exclusionary values and beliefs that America, and therefore, "Americanness" represented.

In the next chapter, I examine how undocumented young adults in Los Angeles and Atlanta challenged dominant anti-immigrant narratives through activism. While undocumented immigrant activists focused primarily on educational access in their respective locales, their activism engaged with notions of Americanness, belonging, and citizenship. I highlight the motivations and constraints that Latinx undocumented young adults faced as they considered engaging in activism. Finally, I show how this process of negotiation is integral to fully understanding the multiple—and sometimes competing—obligations that Latinx undocumented young adults encountered as they transitioned to adulthood.

CHAPTER 5

THE IMMIGRANT BARGAIN EXTENDED

Undocumented Youth Activism

On January 9, 2015, over twenty undocumented students and about thirty documented student allies attended a teach-in at the University of Georgia, one of the three universities in Georgia where undocumented youth are barred from attending because of their legal status. A sign posted on a classroom door read "Desegregation in Progress." Nearly fifty years earlier, on this same date, the University of Georgia officially desegregated and allowed the first African American students to attend the campus. During the teach-in, student activists listened to the experiences of civil rights activists Lonnie King and Loretta Ross. Ms. Ross emphasized, "My first radical act was my parents and I fighting for my right to an education" (Pitti 2015). As in the civil rights movement, *access* to education has been a central issue for the undocumented youth movement. Drawing on the legacy of the civil rights movement, around 2010, undocumented youth activists began to participate in peaceful acts of civil disobedience, which regularly resulted in their arrest. At 5:00 p.m., when campus police ordered participants to leave the classroom or face charges of criminal trespassing, all but nine participants stayed in the classroom. Of those who remained, four were undocumented young people who were ultimately arrested.

Diana, one of the undocumented students who was arrested, explained during an interview at her home over a month later that she was motivated to participate in civil disobedience by the hardship her parents faced migrating to the United States. Through tears, she said, "My parents sacrificed everything for me to have a better life. . . . and for Georgia to take that away, it's just, it's just something that I am not going to allow." As Diana's experience illustrates, children of immigrants, including those who are immigrants themselves, seek to honor their parents' sacrifices both during and after migration to the United States by pursuing a better life. As I discussed in chapter 3, for most of the young people in this book, the path to social mobility and a better life meant getting a college degree and pursuing the doors it would open. While many young people, regardless of their immigration status, aspire to social mobility through a college education, children of immigrants feel a particular commitment to this pathway, motivated by their parents' migration sacrifices, immigrant optimism, and the drive to take advantage of the opportunities the United States offers (Louie 2004). One of these critical opportunities is access to better education, and it is the primary way immigrant parents and their children perceive opportunities for economic and social mobility in the United States (Lee and Zhou 2014).

In his study of Mexican immigrants in New York City, Robert Smith (2006) introduced the concept of keeping the immigrant bargain. In this dynamic, children of immigrants push themselves academically to realize their parents' hopes and dreams for a better life when migrating to the United States. Sociologist Vivian Louie extends our understanding of the immigrant bargain in her study of 1.5- and second-generation Colombian and Dominican children of immigrants and their families. As Louie argues, hope, motivation, and familial support must be coupled with "powerful institutional and other nonfamily support" (Louie 2012, 2) for children of immigrants to realize their college-going dreams. For undocumented immigrants, like the young people in this book, keeping the immigrant bargain presents an even greater challenge precisely because institutional access is limited. Further complicating the pursuit of social mobility is that college access varies widely by where undocumented young people live. Previous research about the undocumented 1.5 generation shows that, despite legal and institutional barriers, undocumented young people and their families also place significant value on realizing their parents' hopes and dreams through education (Cebulko 2014; Enriquez 2011; Gonzales 2011; Abrego and Gonzales 2010; Abrego 2006).

In one of the first studies of the educational aspirations of undocumented immigrant young people, Leisy Abrego (2006) finds that they develop educational aspirations and expectations like most U.S.-born youth; they hope to go to college and start successful careers. Even as their educational trajectories are less certain after high school, during high school, undocumented immigrant youth still harness multiple sources of support to reach their academic goals (Enriquez 2011). Laura Enriquez (2011) finds that the emotional support parents provide through encouragement and motivation is integral for undocumented immigrant youth to continue to and through college. The constant encouragement and motivation parents offer further deepen undocumented youths' emotional commitment to improving their lives through education for themselves and their families. Despite this deep commitment, and especially before the announcement of Deferred Action for Childhood Arrivals (DACA), undocumented immigrant young adults were constrained from fully realizing their educational and career goals because of their legal status. Access to higher education gave rise to the undocumented student movement and has become a central part of the movement's framing and advocacy efforts (Burciaga and Martinez 2017; Enriquez and Saguy 2016). The movement's commitment to advocating for access to higher education reflects the lived experiences of undocumented immigrant youth as they strive for a better future for themselves and their families. As the undocumented student movement has evolved, the connection between education, family, and activism has become intimately intertwined for undocumented youth activists.

In this chapter, I explore how undocumented young people in California and Georgia extended notions of "keeping the immigrant bargain" through participation in undocumented youth activism, with a focus on advocacy for educational access. The nature of this advocacy differed by the challenges faced in each state, underscoring the importance of understanding the role of local contexts in shaping undocumented youth activism (Burciaga and Martinez 2017). Yet, access to higher education was a central issue in both locales. As the undocumented youth movement became more established, young people articulated broader conceptions of activism, and therefore, keeping the immigration bargain. Local organizations and campus groups were the main ways for young people to participate in the movement formally. Yet, in interviews, young people, especially in California, conceptualized their presence in college as a form of resistance or "academic activism," as one participant put it. In Georgia, aspiring activists faced more barriers to formal participation created by the hostile political context and the practicalities of navigating everyday life. Yet, in both locales, young people expressed an implicit understanding that they were keeping the immigrant bargain through school, work, and participation in activism. In the following sections, I unpack how undocumented young people in this study made meaning of the rise of the undocumented youth movement and their relationship to activism. I start by providing a historical analysis of the emergence and evolution of the undocumented youth movement nationally and in California and Georgia. I examine how participation varies *between* and *within* state contexts by identifying various factors, including hostile and welcoming state policies, that shaped participants' understanding of the relationship between their plans for their future, activism, and their families.

The Rise of the Undocumented Youth Movement

Undocumented youth activism is part of a longer legacy of Latinx and immigrant rights activism (Zepeda-Millan 2017; Nicholls 2013; Martinez 2008). As we saw at the beginning of this chapter, it is also profoundly connected to the legacy of the civil rights movement, especially in the U.S. South. The undocumented youth movement burst onto the public scene on May 17, 2010, when four undocumented young people and one citizen ally, all dressed in colorful caps and gowns, marched into Arizona Senator John McCain's office, asking Senator McCain to co-sponsor the Development Relief and Education for Alien Minors (DREAM) Act, which had been introduced regularly since 2001. The five activists refused to leave Senator McCain's office until he agreed to their demands, leading to their arrest. This was a watershed moment that was a part of actions and events across the country during the spring and summer of 2010, including a trek from Florida to Washington, D.C. (referred to as the Trail of Dreams), hunger strikes, and shutting down major streets in cities across the United States, including in Los Angeles and Atlanta. While the movement's emergence in 2010 seemed sudden, for those involved, the shift in strategies and tactics reflected years of movement-building and engagement. It also reflected the growing reality that undocumented youth were no longer political subjects who needed to be spoken for (Nicholls 2013).

During the summer of 2010, undocumented youth activists made two bold moves. The first was to break away from the broader immigrant rights movement advocating for comprehensive immigration reform to push for passage of the DREAM Act as a "stand-alone" bill. Second, drawing inspiration from the lesbian, gay, bisexual, and transgender (LGBT) movement and activists of the civil rights movement, undocumented immigrant youth activists across the country launched a campaign based on undocumented immigrant youth publicly sharing their legal status and engaging in acts of civil disobedience, declaring that they were "undocumented and unafraid" (Muñoz 2015; Nicholls 2013; Unzueta Carrasco and Seif 2014). Alongside public acts of civil disobedience like the May 2010 occupation of Senator McCain's office, campus and community-based groups held "Coming Out of the Shadows" events focused on having undocumented young people share their stories. These events took different shapes and forms but typically included two to three activists who would share what they remembered from their migration journey, how they learned about their undocumented status, and the challenges they faced as undocumented young people. The coming out events, as they came to be known, served multiple purposes, including to help other undocumented young people see people who were like them, to humanize the experience of undocumented youth, and, during the fight for passage of the DREAM Act in 2010, to help others understand the urgency tied to legislative action. While coming out events were an exciting movement development, these events rippled through campus- and community-based undocumented student organizations, the heart of the DREAM movement, as undocumented young adults navigated a new challenge. The opportunity to disclose their status in various public settings, including at Coming Out of the Shadows events. These events reflected a shifting legal consciousness among undocumented young adult activists (Muñoz 2016). Education scholar Susana Muñoz (2015; 2016) argues that, while legal status is somewhat fixed, legal consciousness is a dynamic process of undocumented young adults making sense of their status, especially as they transition into adulthood. A key dimension of this process is negotiating when, how, and to whom to disclose one's status, known as *disclosure management*. As I discussed earlier in this book, undocumented young people developed strategies to disclose their status to institutional agents, including high school counselors or supportive teachers, to gather information and guidance about going to college. This type of one-on-one disclosure was qualitatively different from sharing one's status in a public venue such as a rally on campus or an event out in the community. For undocumented youth who declared they were "undocumented and unafraid," sharing their status in a public setting required that they confront fears related to their legal status, which were ingrained in them as children and were meant to protect themselves and their families. Participation in the movement, however, contextualized these fears as undocumented youth faced them by sharing their story in their communities, participating in marches and rallies and, for a few, participating in acts of civil disobedience. As more undocumented young people shared their status and the repercussions they feared, such as getting deported, did not happen, the legal consciousness of undocumented young people shifted. Declaring oneself "undocumented and unafraid" became an act of empowered disclosure, connecting undocumented young people to one another and challenging harmful narratives about undocumented immigrants (Muñoz 2016).

After months of intense action, in early December 2010, the DREAM Act successfully passed the House of Representatives, a significant victory for undocumented youth and the broader immigrant rights movement that struggled to get any movement on bills that included a pathway to citizenship (Chishti et al. 2010). But two weeks later, the Senate filibustered a vote on the DREAM Act, effectively killing the bill. Although the DREAM Act's failure was crushing for undocumented youth activists, the momentum built in 2010 gave rise to a vibrant movement. Rather than squash further activism, the same activists continued to push for a solution, leading to the 2012 introduction of the DACA program. In addition, the movement shifted focus to expanding rights and access at the state and local levels.

How undocumented young people in California and Georgia, both activists and nonactivists, made sense of the rise of the undocumented youth movement and opportunities for activist participation highlights the importance of legal ecologies in this aspect of undocumented young people's lives. During interviews, undocumented young people discussed the influence of layered and intersectional policy contexts at the federal and state level, and the relational nature of disclosing their status in a public venue. The restrictive educational context in Georgia required direct action, but the hostile political context made this challenging for undocumented young people in the state. In California, a welcoming context coupled with the introduction of DACA eased pressure on some undocumented young people and created space for "academic activism." In both states, undocumented young people were proud of the strides the movement made, including the introduction of DACA, which helped many participants keep the immigrant bargain and honor their parents' migration sacrifices. In both regions, undocumented young people faced practical constraints that limited participation in activism, such as focusing on school or working. Even with the introduction of DACA, expanded college access remained a key issue in both states.

Undocumented Youth Activism in California and Georgia

College access laws not only shaped the individual trajectory of undocumented young adults but also influenced the goals and strategies of the undocumented youth movement in each state. California has long been a hub for undocumented student activism, facilitated by educational gains for undocumented young people. In contrast, Georgia's restrictive educational policies motivated the emergence of a vibrant undocumented youth movement. Understanding the nature and character of undocumented youth activism in each state helps to paint a more complete picture of the context undocumented young people navigated as they contemplated whether they would participate in activism.

Undocumented and Unafraid in the Golden State

In January 2001, then California Governor Gray Davis signed Assembly Bill (AB) 540, which allowed eligible undocumented youth to pay in-state tuition at public colleges and universities. AB 540 was the second in-state residency tuition policy enacted in the United States and resulted from an advocacy partnership between legislators and undocumented youth

activists (Seif 2004). Undocumented youth activism in California, however, started in the 1980s with the formation of the Leticia A. Network.
The Network was a group of concerned educators and undocumented
students who legally challenged the classification of "nonresident" for
tuition purposes (Seif 2004). Realizing that the lawsuit could not move
forward without undocumented youth participation, the Leticia A. Network worked closely with undocumented youth to share the challenges
they faced trying to go to college while still protecting students' identities. Through the turbulent 1990s, which saw the passage of California's
Proposition 187, and into the 2000s, undocumented youth activists and
their citizen allies wrestled with the question of whether to have undocumented young people share their story and, in doing so, reveal their
legal status. At the time, the consequences of sharing their legal status
at legislative hearings and in public venues were unknown. Yet undocumented young people in California knew it would be difficult to appeal to
the public without putting a human face to their challenges. During the
fight for California's in-state tuition law, AB 540, undocumented youth
activists organized with the help of Latinx nonprofit organizations, setting the stage for continued mobilization (Seif 2004).

The fight for in-state tuition in California had the unintended conse-
quence of further mobilizing undocumented youth (Abrego 2008). Following the passage of AB 540 in 2001, undocumented student clubs and
organizations sprouted on college campuses across California (Abrego
2008; Nicholls 2013). Abrego (2008) suggests that the AB 540 law had
important instrumental and constitutive effects on undocumented youth.
Beyond providing undocumented youth the opportunity to pay in-state
tuition, the law also provided undocumented youth with a socially ac-
ceptable identity, that of "AB 540" students. As opposed to the stigma-
tized "undocumented" or "illegal" label, identifying as an AB 540 student
not only gave undocumented young people a greater sense of confidence
and willingness to seek out institutional support from financial aid counselors and professors but also made it easier for undocumented youth
to find one another to form campus-based groups (Abrego 2008). It is
important to note, however, that this organizing was not without fear.
During this early period of student mobilization, undocumented youth
activists considered even the most mundane social movement activities,
such as forming or joining an organization, calling Congress to pass a

bill, or participating in a march or rally, fraught with uncertainty. Maximiliano, who was an "early riser" in the undocumented student movement in California, recounted during an interview:

> We went through this whole, it took us probably two months to decide whether we were going to start an AB 540 group or not. And we decided we were. So, we started the group, and that's when we came out, and that's when we started telling people, you know, we're AB 540. Because we didn't want to use undocumented. . . . Because you never know if people are, have good intentions or bad intentions.

Despite this fear and uncertainty, throughout the 2000s, undocumented youth in California continued to build a dynamic movement, and activists and organizations based in Southern California played a prominent role in the national movement and in Dream Summer 2010. Spurred in part by the sudden passing of prominent California-based activists Tam Tran and Cinthya Felix in 2010, undocumented youth activists in Southern California organized several impactful events during Dream Summer, including a hunger strike, shutting down a major thoroughfare in Los Angeles, and several Coming Out of the Shadows events across the region (Wong et al. 2012). Tam (who grew up in Orange County) and Cinthya (who grew up in Los Angeles) were graduates of the University of California, Los Angeles (UCLA), where they were integral in campus organizing for undocumented students. After graduation from UCLA, Tam and Cinthya left Southern California for graduate school on the East Coast—Cinthya to be the first undocumented master's student in public health at Columbia University's School of Public Health, and Tam to attend a PhD program in American Studies at Brown University. Undocumented youth activists in Southern California were inspired by Tam and Cinthya, who were unafraid to pursue their educational goals and advocacy for the undocumented student community. At Coming Out of the Shadows Events in Southern California, undocumented young people declared they were "undocumented and unafraid." By 2010, undocumented activists in California were firmly out of the shadows, challenging public narratives that painted the broader undocumented immigrant population as hiding and generally fearful of engaging in public life. In many ways, the daily lives of undocumented immigrant youth were at odds with this public narrative as they and their families had learned to navigate going to college and working. The lives of Tam and Cinthya reflected this reality as they did not let their status hold them back from pursuing their educational goals. For undocumented youth in Southern California, declaring they were "undocumented and unafraid" was also a call to action, encouraging undocumented young people to advocate for access to higher education and a pathway to citizenship through the passage of the DREAM Act.

By the summer of 2010, the undocumented youth movement in California focused on passing the DREAM Act and securing state financial aid for undocumented students. When the DREAM Act failed to pass in 2010, organizers in the state turned their attention to passing the California Dream Act (AB 130 and AB 131). Governor Jerry Brown signed the California Dream Act in 2012, granting state and institutional financial aid to undocumented students enrolled in public colleges and universities. The law took effect in January 2013 and had been a statewide movement goal since the passage of AB 540 in 2001. The California Dream Act radically shifted the educational opportunities available to the Latinx undocumented young adults I interviewed in California because, for many, it coincided with their transition out of high school. While the California Dream Act was a significant victory for undocumented youth in California, in other states, like Georgia, policymakers have taken a different stance and are actively excluding undocumented youth. In the next section, I discuss the emergence and current state of the undocumented youth movement in Georgia.

Undocumented and Unafraid in the Nuevo South

In 2010, Jessica Colotl was an undergraduate student at Kennesaw State University, a public college located in the metropolitan Atlanta area. On her way home from school, Jessica was pulled over for a minor traffic violation, but she did not have a driver's license because she was undocumented. Despite having immigrated with her family when she was ten years old and spending half her life in Georgia, under the Secure Communities program, Jessica was referred to Immigration and Customs Enforcement. She was sent to a federal immigration detention center in Alabama. Her arrest and the deportation proceedings that followed were part of a larger firestorm in Georgia around issues related to undocumented immigrants. One of the key public reactions to her arrest was outrage that Jessica was paying in-state tuition at Kennesaw State. This was despite the passage in 2010 of the Georgia Board of Regents Policy 4.3.4, requiring that undocumented immigrants pay out-of-state tuition. The saga played out on local TV and significant coverage was on the local Spanish television stations. The Georgia immigrant rights community rallied around Jessica, and she was eventually released from detention and returned to Kennesaw State as a student paying out-of-state tuition.

I center my discussion about the emergence of the undocumented youth movement in Georgia around the arrest of Jessica Colotl because, for many of the undocumented young adults I interviewed, it was a defining moment. For some, it was the first time they learned about the Board of Regents' policies and realized that they may not be able to attend college. Her arrest signaled a broader trend they had sensed was happening, an increase in anti-immigrant sentiment. The Board of Regents policies were passed around the same time as House Bill (HB) 87, a "show me your papers" law that included a range of harsh provisions aimed at the undocumented immigrant community. For many of the participants from Georgia, the Board of Regents policy had the most acute impact on their day-to-day lives. As Saul stated during our interview,

> It was on the local news. . . . I think it was when that girl from Kennesaw got pulled over and that's when it all started . . . and they found out she was going to Kennesaw State as an undocumented student . . . and that's where all these anti-immigrant folks like started freaking out. They were like, "Oh these illegals are coming to our schools," and that's when the politicians were like, "Oh we got to do something about this." That's really where the ban came out of. That's how I saw it.

Although the ban took effect the year before Jessica's arrest in 2010, the media coverage of her fight to stay in the country and to finish college made "the ban" a reality. Because of this, ending the Board of Regents policies became a central organizing issue for undocumented youth activists in Georgia. The ban coincided with heightened activism around passing the DREAM Act in 2010; undocumented young adults in Georgia were already mobilizing to pass the DREAM Act. The ban provided a state-level focal point for their activism and became the central mobilizing issue following the failure of the DREAM Act. Unlike activists in California, undocumented youth in Georgia did not have the central organizing space that college campuses provide. Nevertheless, community-based undocumented student organizations mobilized in the major cities, including Atlanta, Athens, and Savannah. Undocumented youth created dynamic spaces for activism that have fueled the growth of the undocumented student movement in Georgia. A key community-based space for undocumented activism in the state is Freedom University, a grassroots nonprofit organization based in the Atlanta area.

In response to the ban, in 2011, faculty from the University of Georgia, located in Athens about ninety miles outside of Atlanta, started an underground university modeled after the Freedom Schools in the Deep South (Soltis 2015). Freedom University offers tuition-free, college-level classes, and movement leadership training to undocumented young adults in the state. Professors from colleges and universities around the state, including the University of North Georgia, Emory University, and the University of Georgia, meet once a week in an undisclosed location and, over the course of four hours, undocumented students take a range of courses including *Race, Immigration, and Incarceration in the United States*; *History of Social Movements in Mexico*; and *Introduction to Ethnic Studies*. In addition to these courses, students can participate in a college preparatory program that includes preparing applications to attend college primarily at out-of-state institutions, applying for scholarships, and navigating college life. Trivette and English (2017) find that the college preparation focus of Freedom University has facilitated the college-going pathways of undocumented young people in the state.

Although Freedom University is not formally accredited, scholar Laura Emiko Soltis argues that the work of Freedom University is "education for liberation, not accreditation" (Soltis 2015, 32). This model of liberatory education facilitates students' understanding of their own inherent humanity and how their struggle as undocumented young people in a hostile context is connected to other struggles and is part of a legacy of existence as resistance. This focus on rigorous college-level coursework, creating a safe space, and developing a critical consciousness means that Freedom University has become a conduit for young people to be a part of mobilization through community-based organizations like the Georgia Undocumented Youth Alliance (GUYA), which has been a key site for activism in the state. When I was conducting my fieldwork, GUYA was in the process of regrouping as core members had left the state for college, had recently become parents, or were focusing their energies on navigating their futures. Not all students who attend Freedom University become involved in undocumented youth activism, and as I found during my time in Atlanta, this was because of other constraints, including the need to work or family responsibilities. Those who did get involved developed leadership skills they could discuss should they choose to apply to college (Trivette and English 2017).

Despite a hostile context and fewer undocumented student organizations, the undocumented youth movement in Georgia is very active. Undocumented youth activists have taken a dual-purpose approach to increasing higher education *in* Georgia, focusing on increasing access to higher education in-state at both public and private institutions. For example, an ally student group at Emory University successfully advocated for the university to commit to admitting and fully funding five undocumented students per year, starting in the 2015–2016 school year. There are also ally groups at Kennesaw State University and Georgia State University highlighting the undocumented student movement's primary focus on the issue of increasing college access to the state's public colleges and universities. Using tactics like those of the larger undocumented youth movement, since 2011, undocumented youth activists and citizen allies in Georgia have regularly participated in acts of civil disobedience. These have included disrupting Board of Regents meetings, shutting down traffic in Atlanta, and occupying a classroom at the University of Georgia, an action I described at the beginning of this chapter. Contrary to the intended impact of the state's hostile laws, some but not all undocumented young adults in Georgia are actively resisting these efforts through activist participation.

In the sections that follow, I explore the ways Latinx undocumented young adults made sense of activist participation in Los Angeles and Atlanta. While many of the undocumented young adults I interviewed in both places were involved to some degree in the local undocumented student movements in their communities, many were not, reflecting undocumented young adults' perceptions about what it means to keep the immigrant bargain, that is, to recognize their parents' migration sacrifices and legal vulnerability here in the United States. For some, this meant advocating for educational access, and for others, it meant focusing on school or work. Across both locales, undocumented young people shared that they were grateful for the gains made through activism, including the DACA program.

"Coming Out" in Accommodating and Hostile Contexts

To understand how and why some undocumented young adults mobilize, it is necessary to first understand the specific challenges related to social movement participation that are tied to legal status. In both California and Georgia, most of the undocumented young people I interviewed grew up aware of their legal status. Several, though not all, remembered coming to the United States, and their migration stories ranged from mundane to harrowing. For many, this experience of crossing, whether by land or air, was the first discovery of the clandestine nature of their existence in the United States. Their childhood experiences, though, were punctuated by contradictory moments of belonging and exclusion. While many described elementary and middle school primarily as sites of belonging, undocumented young adults in both locales also described discrete experiences of exclusion during their childhood years. During our interview, Vanessa, who migrated with her family to Georgia on a tourist visa, explained that she knew they were undocumented because of the way her parents acted. When I asked her to describe how she knew, she recalled a state of constant vigilance: "It was just like always fear. Just always looking out for police when we were driving or making sure we weren't out at a certain time of the day." Hugo, who migrated to metropolitan Los Angeles with his mother and his sister, echoed Vanessa's sense of growing up in fear: "They told us not share it [his status] with anybody. As a result, fear was instilled from a young age of my status and my identity as well."

Despite growing up with this fear, undocumented young adults in California and Georgia developed strategies during high school for sharing their status with trusted friends and occasionally teachers or counselors. However, I noted a significant difference in the "coming out" stories of

Latinx undocumented young adults in California and Georgia. In the metropolitan Los Angeles area, the sheer size of the undocumented Latinx community, coupled with a more welcoming environment, made it slightly easier for undocumented young adults to disclose their status to others, *especially* as they approached the college application process. In contrast, young people in the Atlanta area reported feeling like the only undocumented student in their high school. They reported few opportunities to disclose their status to friends or teachers. This is in stark contrast to previous research about the integral role of these institutional agents in providing key social capital and connections both to colleges and universities but also to possible mobilization opportunities (Gonzales 2016; Enriquez 2011).

This sense of isolation led participants in Georgia to avoid seeking help during the college application process and closed off opportunities to find support from other undocumented youth or guidance counselors and teachers. During interviews conducted in 2010 with undocumented student activists in Southern California, I found that their experiences of sharing their legal status one-on-one with trusted confidants other than family and friends comprised an important part of the process of "becoming an activist." Similarly, Enriquez and Saguy (2016) suggest that successful private experiences of disclosing status open the door to disclosing status in more public settings—in the context of activism, for instance. I expected that undocumented young adults in Georgia would be less likely to feel comfortable sharing their status, both in general and in activist spaces, because of the hostile climate and fewer opportunities during high school to become comfortable with their undocumented identity.

This was indeed the case for some undocumented young adults in Georgia, but I also found that others were actively engaged in the undocumented youth movement in the state. In addition, I found that, in California, where youth have multiple opportunities to successfully disclose their status, the undocumented youth I interviewed were less engaged in the broader undocumented youth movement in the state, which became multifaceted. Following the passage of in-state and institutional financial aid, California-based undocumented youth organizations turned their attention to antideportation campaigns (Patler and Gonzales 2015), ending the school-to-deportation pipeline (Burciaga 2015) and advocating for the expansion of state benefits such as healthcare (Plascencia et al. 2015).

The most interesting pattern that emerged from the experiences of undocumented young adults in both Los Angeles and Atlanta, including participants and nonparticipants, is their perception and understanding of *how* their commitment to their families impacted their participation in activism. Whether undocumented young adults were "active" or not in the movement, they all made sense of their participation or nonparticipation through the lens of what it meant to give back to their families and, therefore, keep the immigrant bargain. The starkest contrast to emerge, then, was between undocumented youth activists in Georgia and campus-based activists in California, as both groups viewed themselves as keeping the immigrant bargain. Within each state, and especially in Georgia, obligations such as working and helping with siblings, both activities connected to family, also influenced whether undocumented young adults simply had the time to participate in activism.

Keeping the Immigrant Bargain in California and Georgia
Undocumented Young Adults and Academic Activism in California

Because they were enrolled in college, respondents in California were involved primarily in undocumented student organizations on their campuses; this was due in part to the incomplete sense of belonging they felt because of their legal status. Respondents viewed this involvement on campus as an important part of the undocumented student movement, but some hesitated to call it activism. While the undocumented student movement started on college campuses in California, the shift in the larger DREAM movement toward direct action, including hunger strikes and acts of civil disobedience, also shifted undocumented young adults' understanding of "activism." Imelda, who was enrolled in a four-year university and was a member of an undocumented student advocate group that planned an immigration awareness event on campus, cautioned: "I wouldn't consider myself an activist, yet . . . I've participated in small things, but they've never been in an activist space." Jessica, also enrolled at a four-year university and involved in the undocumented student or-ganization on her campus, echoed Imelda's sentiment when reflecting on her activism: "I feel like I am a low-key activist. I definitely focus on school way more than I do activism." Both Imelda and Jessica articulated the prevalent understanding among undocumented youth about the na-ture of activism in the current historical moment; they both believed that being an "activist" meant going out and protesting in the streets. The significant and rapid shift in the tactics and strategies employed by the undocumented youth movement may have had the unintended conse-quence of narrowly circumscribing what constitutes "activism." Respon-dents in California understood this brand of activism to be a significant time commitment that was at odds with the priority they placed on their schooling.

This was not just a perception, however. Xavier, who was a transfer student at a four-year university, revealed that his early involvement in the undocumented student movement impacted his education during community college:

> I took a break for about a long while after probably 2011. I dedicated a lot of my time to these two communities [the undocumented and LGBTQ communities] and it takes a lot of time, that's why I was at [Greater LA Community College] for, I think four years, which was longer than I ex-pected. I really had pressure from my family, too: "When are you going to transfer? When is that going to happen?" They never said, "You need to stop your activism. That's distracting you," or "That's bad," or anything. It was just, "You need to transfer. You need to get your priorities straight and figure out a way to balance your time" or what-not.

As a first-year transfer student at his "dream school," Xavier made the conscious decision to focus his efforts on school despite encourage-ment from university staff and faculty to get involved in various campus groups. He elaborated,

> I think I'm still looking for something. . . . I met a really good friend; his name is Eddie. He's really active in the community, but I think he was also taking a break. He's like, "It's good to take a break. It's good to recharge and

find yourself," but he's started getting involved again. I just became really busy the last month or so with midterms and final papers.

While Xavier did not rule out getting involved again on his new campus, he was cautious about the idea and was prioritizing his studies. During our interview, he stated that it made him feel "selfish," but that he also felt an internal pressure to finish school, especially because he took four years to transfer from community college to a four-year university. Beyond the shifting idea of what "activism" means within the broader context of the undocumented youth movement, respondents in California stated that school was their priority because of the challenges of getting to college as an undocumented young person, even within a relatively positive policy climate.

The day-to-day struggle of negotiating college as an undocumented student forced many undocumented young adults in California to prioritize their education over activism. Alejandra was involved with her campus undocumented student organization and wanted to be "hardcore," attending protests and events. She shared,

> I started small with [undocumented student organization]. I started by being the treasurer because, back in high school, I was good with sales and stuff. It was like, if I could help in that point, like go ahead. My other friends are really crazy. They go to protests all the time. I wish I could go, but every time they go, I have a class.

Alejandra was building her identity as an activist by attending events and protests, as long as they did not conflict with her class schedule. She shared with her mom that she was planning to attend a May Day event where police would be present. Her mom was "really scared" and advised her to, "Be careful. Don't get close to them. Do nothing to get their attention." Although Alejandra pushed back a bit, telling her mom that they would be there protesting peacefully, she elaborated that,

> I feel like maybe I need a little more knowledge of the movement. It's mostly school. Right now, I'm like, "I want to graduate." Any little thing that could mess me up, could potentially mess me, I can't afford to mess up.

Having a good GPA is what brought me into having so many scholarships, so I don't want to mess it up.

Alejandra was determined to finish college so she could have a career and independence, and this meant prioritizing attending class. Reflecting on her mom's life and gender dynamics, she elaborated,

I've always seen my mom doing little jobs here and there. I don't want to be like that. It sucks that she had to go through it, and her mom too. and so on and so forth, but I want to be that stop and be like, "Yeah, okay, that's it. This thing can't go on anymore." I know many guys are against their wife working or whatever, and I'm like, "no" I want to work and do something for myself. I want to be able to have a career and be like, "Look, mom, I did it. It stopped." That's it. Now, hopefully, my kids continue, and then their kids and whatever. I'm the oldest from both sides of my family.

Like Alejandra, participants in California were motivated to do well in school in part because they grew up watching their parents struggle because of their legal status, lack of formal education, and related lack of career opportunities. Undocumented young adults in California made sense of "smaller" involvement on their campus as part of a larger plan to prioritize their education and eventually give back to their parents. They engaged in "low-key" participation not out of fear of deportation or similar uncertainty but a concern about the time activism might take away from their other responsibilities, including school and work. For example, Luz shared that her first quarter in college was challenging: "It was very hard for me, time management. I wasn't good at it; it was my first quarter, so it was very tough." But as she managed her time better, she was able to get involved with a campus-based program for undocumented students and was organizing a graduation ceremony with eight other undocumented students. She described the challenging time they had recruiting participants and how she learned that there were only four hundred undocumented students at her college. As the time for the graduation rehearsal approached, she learned more about the challenges and triumphs of her fellow undocumented students:

We requested for information from the participants saying, "Send us pictures that represent your journey of education, a small thank you letter, why you would like to join this ceremony." We read a lot. . . . I read a lot of interesting stories; you have students who have a family and balance both things and are still getting the higher education. People who live with their grandparents, people who don't even have a family supporting them, and I felt like that kind of reinforced everything, like why we're doing it.

On the day of the rehearsal, Luz shared that eighty students showed up, and even though it was a "small group," I sensed that it was meaningful, and she felt like she was building something for future students.

The majority of the undocumented young adults that I interviewed in California were working part-time to help finance their education and support themselves while they were in school. While they were grateful for the opportunity to receive state and institutional aid, many still needed to work to pay for books, food, and other expenses. For many, this left little time to dedicate to the type of activism they imagined would make a difference. Maria, who was a leader in the undocumented student organization on her campus and regularly represented her campus at statewide meetings for undocumented students, stated:

A lot of my activism does take place on campus. . . . I feel like activism is . . . it varies. I think I try to be as good of an academic activist as possible. It's hard to get through all those readings, but I do believe that's one form of activism is studying because . . . you study, you graduate, you get the job that you worked hard to get, and you give back to your community. I think those are good-hearted people, and that's what they do: they give back.

Maria and other undocumented young adults in California viewed their academic achievement as not only giving back to their family but also eventually creating a pathway to give back to their community—A form of academic activism. Meanwhile, as undocumented young adults in California were keeping the immigrant bargain according to the more traditional conceptualization of this idea, respondents in Georgia also constructed a narrative wherein they were keeping the immigrant bargain. In the next section, I examine mobilization among respondents in Georgia, both participants and nonparticipants.

Keeping the Immigrant Bargain in Georgia

At the beginning of this chapter, I introduced Diana, a soft-spoken young woman with long black hair and a huge smile. During my time in Atlanta, I was Diana's volunteer driver; every weekend for nearly three months, I took her and other students from their homes to Freedom University. During our car rides, I came to realize, though, that Diana's soft voice hid her power and commitment to the undocumented student movement. Diana graduated from high school in 2012, the second year the ban was in place. She excelled in high school and was an active member of the school band. She was also in a serious relationship with a citizen, and they were planning on going to college together and, according to Diana, "making it more serious." Tragically, her partner died a month before high school graduation. For Diana, his death, in conjunction with being undocumented, profoundly impacted her life, and it was apparent during our interview that it was difficult for her to disentangle the precise cause of the deep depression she fell into following her high school graduation. During our interview, she confided in me about the very dark period she experienced in 2012 when she finished high school:

> We were setting up a future together; it was just, we were building it and then all of a sudden, like, the rug is pulled from under my feet. I couldn't go to school, I couldn't work, I couldn't drive; it's just like my life was not going in the direction I wanted to, and it was so . . . frustrating and I just wanted to give up.

From 2012 until 2014, Diana was housebound and severely depressed. In 2014, her father found a newspaper article about Freedom University and encouraged Diana to attend a class. He told her, "You have to go here, they help students get to college. We know that you've been having difficulty and it's not your fault, it's just we can't pay for it, and there's just so many other factors." Diana, who was terrified to disclose her status to teachers and counselors in high school, was worried that it was a ploy to lure undocumented immigrants. So, when she arrived in class that first Sunday, she overcame her nervousness and was instead empowered by what she found. As evidence of how far Diana had come, during one of the classes that I stayed to observe, the group had a lip sync battle to build community among students. Diana, who described herself as "extremely shy," performed Bruno Mars's "Uptown Funk" and, on our car ride home, she admitted to me that it was a huge accomplishment for her to get out there; this was a testament not only to Diana's personal resolve but also to the safe and empowering space Freedom University cultivated for undocumented youth (Muñoz and Espino 2017; Soltis 2015).

During my time in Atlanta, Diana was one of the most prominent student activists at Freedom University and in the undocumented student movement in Georgia. Part of her path to mobilization included participating in the January 9, 2015, sit-in action at the University of Georgia. Her motivation was rooted in her parents' sacrifice: "My parents sacrificed everything for me to have a better life . . . and for Georgia to take that away, it's just, it's just something that I am not going to allow." But like other undocumented youth activists in Georgia, she demonstrated a commitment to the broader undocumented youth community:

> I was like, "You know you got to do this" [be arrested]. Because the endpoint is not me just getting the education. It's about everyone getting education. . . . Because I know my sister wants to stay here, like, it's not fair that I have these amazing opportunities. I got to go visit these schools . . . and every other undocumented student in Georgia doesn't have the amazing opportunity that I did. And so, I want to be able to open up that for them. And I know that a lot of them don't want to leave because their parents are undocumented. It's just all these issues that would be better if they just went to school here in Georgia.

Diana, who had traveled to visit colleges like Dartmouth, Smith, and Hampshire as a part of Freedom University's fall college tour, realized that her experience was unique compared with other undocumented youth in Georgia, like her sister. In addition, as Diana implied, the continued legal precarity of undocumented youths' parents in a hostile state could preclude them from going out of state for college. Other undocumented youth who were engaged in the student movement in Georgia shared similar sentiments. They were motivated not only to change the laws in Georgia so they could get an education but also to improve things for others, including their siblings. For instance, Vanessa made peace with attending college out of state, but she also had a younger sibling who was undocumented, and she wanted him to have the option to attend an in-state college. Thus, she was motivated both by her parents and future generations, including her brother:

> You know my mom is like, I didn't finish high school, your dad didn't finish high school, you have to be the first one in our family to go to college, to do something. We didn't come here, bust our ass for nothing. I'm like, you're right, you're right.

Marco, who was an only child and did not want to attend an out-of-state college because he needed to be close to his parents, stated that he was also motivated to participate in activism because of "future generations." During our interview, he explained:

> One of the reasons why I do this is to help future generations that are going to be illegal. Because you know, here in the U.S., it's always made target of one group at a time, and right now, unfortunately, it's us, the Latinos . . . if we can change things now and make them better for future generations to come.

For undocumented youth activists in Georgia, involvement in activism was motivated both by a sense of duty to their parents and by a commitment to the broader undocumented youth community in the state, who may not be as connected as these young people are. While the immediate benefit would be for them and their families, they also exhibited a collective consciousness about their activism.

For undocumented young adults in Georgia who were not actively involved in the undocumented student movement in the state, the biggest constraint was time. For nonactivists, work, which often occupied more than forty to fifty hours per week, left little time for activism. In these young people's perceptions, working provided two related ways of keeping the immigrant bargain: First, in the short term, undocumented young adults worked to contribute to their family's expenses, including rent, food, and other household supplies. When I interviewed Ines, who graduated from high school in 2013, she stated: "I've been working since I was fourteen, and I've always contributed at home with my mom and my dad." Ines was referred to me by a student at Freedom University.

While she was very enthusiastic about participating, at the time of our interview, she was working sixty to seventy hours per week. I had an extremely difficult time coordinating the interview with her. After several texts back and forth, we managed to conduct the interview at her place of work between two shifts. She apologized for the scheduling challenges and explained that, besides home, this was the place where she spent the most time. During our interview, she expressed the fact that she felt her life had stalled:

> I've been working for about two years now here after I graduated. You feel really like you want to do more, but at the same time, you feel like you can't. It's just like, you're just there. It becomes the same cycle. You feel like you're being trapped in the same cycle; you graduate, and you just work. Even though you don't want to do that.

During our interview, she expressed an interest in participating in activism, but her primary concern was her work schedule. She continued:

> After so many things that I went through, I kind of just laid low for a little while, just started working, just regular. I didn't really get much into contact with any other groups until now, when I heard about that [Freedom University]. I want to start. I'm nervous about work, because I actually work weekends, I work twelve hours. The other days, I work fifteen. I live here more than I live at home; I work here a lot.

Despite an interest in getting involved, Ines's financial obligations to her family required that she work many hours per week and prevented her from participating in Freedom University.

In addition, undocumented young adults who worked did so because they were saving to eventually attend college, but this impacted their availability to participate in activism. Elena graduated from high school in 2014. She wanted to attend Georgia State University, located in the Atlanta metropolitan area, and was academically qualified. While she could not attend Georgia State because it was one of the institutions undocumented young people were banned from, she was accepted to Oglethorpe University, a private university in the Atlanta area. Still, she could not attend because the financial aid package they offered did not cover the whole cost. She hoped to be able to eventually attend Oglethorpe if she could save enough money to pay the out-of-pocket expense. She was working at a bakery and described the number of hours she worked per week as "pretty low, about thirty-five hours per week." When I interviewed Elena in February, she mentioned that, during the Christmas rush, she worked eighteen hours on certain days; some weeks, she lost track of how much she worked, but it felt like "one hundred hours." This was Elena's second job since she graduated from high school, and with more steady work and a more mature sense of her finances, she had been able to save $7,000 that she planned to use toward college. Although she had recently started attending Freedom University and enjoyed the classes, her work schedule prevented her from participating in activism. Even her attendance at Freedom University depended on her work schedule, which varied weekly. During our interview, she shared, "At the moment, I don't consider myself an activist, but Freedom University pushed me towards fighting for my rights," and she elaborated that being at Freedom University helped her to feel more confident with sharing her story in public. Like Elena, work was the main reason Nancy was unable to attend Freedom University, which many young people saw as a first step toward movement participation. She shared, "My work schedule is Monday through Friday, and I work doubles on Saturday night. Then I only get Sunday off." Nancy's mom, who worked cleaning houses, and her dad, who worked as a janitor, also only had Sundays off, and as she described, during the week, she may go days without seeing her parents, but "Sunday is that one day where we're all there either in the mornings or in the afternoons. We're all there." While she admired the work of activists in the area, she felt that, unless she could be 100 percent, she could not be involved. She shared,

> I think it's amazing. I know it's not very big. There has to be that one group of people that push and fight. It's like Martin Luther King. If he wasn't there to push and fight, nothing would have happened. I completely 100 percent support them. But my schedule, I don't have time for the homework and stuff.

Like Nancy, many undocumented young people in the Atlanta area balanced the knowledge that, even with DACA, laws and policies in the state needed to change, and activism was a route for change. But other obligations like work often prevented their participation, reflecting the salience of their legal ecologies for movement participation.

Conclusion

The rise of the undocumented youth movement in 2010 profoundly changed how both the public and undocumented youth understood the relationship between their legal status and activism. The emergence of strategies and tactics, including hunger strikes, marches, rallies, and sit-ins, empowered undocumented young people, both those who considered themselves activists and those who did not. However, undocumented young people's legal ecologies significantly shaped individual activist participation. At the federal level, the introduction of DACA in 2012 opened doors for young people and eased pressure as they navigated the transition to and through adulthood. In California, DACA, in combination with the passage of the California Dream Act, created the space for young people to focus on their education. As Maria shared, she considered this a form of academic activism. Xavier, who had a firsthand understanding of the time and commitment that activism could take, was taking a break from activism to immerse himself in his studies at his dream college. For these young people, focusing on graduating from college was a meaningful way to honor their parents' sacrifices.

In Georgia, the exclusionary educational context gave rise to a vibrant movement. While many undocumented young people found entrée into the movement through the safe space of Freedom University, Freedom University's primary purpose has always been to be a "safe space where students can come out of the shadows, continue their education, and build relationships in a community of undocumented youth," (Soltis 2015, 28). As undocumented young people developed a critical consciousness, some chose to become further involved. These young activists were motivated both by the injustice of not being able to attend college and by the possibility of making a difference for future generations in the state. At the time of the writing of this book, Regents Policies 4.1.6 and 4.3.4 still stand, excluding undocumented young people from attending the top three colleges in the state and forcing them to pay out-of-state tuition at any public college or university. Despite the long-standing ban, undocumented immigrants in the state of Georgia, including undocumented immigrant youth, continue to advocate for a more just place. For young people who did not consider themselves activists, time was the major factor constraining involvement, even as they appreciated the gains made by the movement. For these young people, the hostile context in concert with DACA meant increased responsibility to work to meet goals such as saving for college, purchasing a car, or contributing to their family's household income. In these ways, undocumented young people who were not activists were keeping a variation of the immigrant bargain, that is, honoring their parents' sacrifices by moving forward in the face of a hostile and exclusionary context.

CONCLUSION

Toward the end of our two-hour interview, David, who had a good sense of humor throughout the interview, reflected on where he saw himself in the next three to five years. He was working the night shift at a food distribution company in the metropolitan Atlanta area, not quite where he thought he would be when he was in high school. He shared,

> I see myself in the next five years in some sort of college. I am not going to say university or technical college because I don't know, to be honest . . . I guess still living in the United States . . . but if I'm twenty-five and I don't know what I'm doing with my life, I'll return to Mexico and do something.

He hoped to be in college but did not know exactly how that would happen. Would he be enrolled at a two-year (e.g., technical) college or a four-year university? When I interviewed David, he should have been in his second year of college; instead, he had been working at a series of jobs since graduating from high school, including as a server, with his mother at a poultry plant and, most recently, at a construction company. David's mom pushed him to get a different job because the construction company did not ask for the work permit that he got through the Deferred Action for Childhood Arrivals (DACA) program. She was worried that the government would see that he was not using the work permit and take it away. Thus, he was working from 11:00 p.m. to 7:00 a.m. at the food distribution company and contemplating his next move and what his future held. In the short term, he was considering moving to Florida for the summer to work at a resort with a friend and deciding what to do after that. If he did not know what he was doing with his life in five years' time, he would consider returning to Mexico. In contrast, Miriam, who was in her second year of college at a four-year public institution in the metropolitan Los Angeles area, confided that her future plans included eventually entering law school. She shared,

> I plan my life a lot, so I have different plans. Like, plan A, plan B, plan C, and everything after that, but I think if there's nothing I can do about the whole reform, I'm probably going to end up just going to a university, a law school, here because I can practice here in California. I guess I would do that, but I wouldn't be content because I'm still stuck.

Conveying her knowledge about the California Supreme Court holding allowing noncitizens to apply for professional licenses, including law licenses, she planned to practice law in California. Miriam also conveyed resentment about feeling "stuck" in California, despite the relative certainty that she would eventually get a college degree, promising social and economic mobility but not necessarily the freedom she hoped for.

I started this book with a question: What role, if any, do state immigration laws and policies play in the lives of Latinx undocumented young people in two distinct contexts of reception? While Miriam and David have divergent social mobility trajectories, they expressed surprisingly similar feelings of uncertainty as they navigated the transition through adulthood. What might explain this? In this book, I have shown that, while state laws and policies are a key mediating factor in the lives of Latinx undocumented young adults, the impact of these laws and policies needs to be understood within the broader legal ecologies of undocumented young adults' lives. Contrasting David's and Miriam's plans for their futures highlights the way undocumented young people's legal ecologies shape their educational and economic outcomes and the possibilities they envision for themselves. While they expressed a similar sense of uncertainty about what their futures held, at that specific moment, their futures were qualitatively different. Miriam was set to graduate from college in two years, poised to enter law school. David, on the other hand, even with DACA, was uncertain about how to make his educational goals a reality. Ultimately, he was considering returning to Mexico. Miriam's and David's divergent trajectories show how Latinx undocumented young adults occupy a unique sociolegal position shaped by intersecting social forces. Understanding these dynamics as legal ecologies is a way of conceptualizing the dialogic nature of federal immigration laws and policies, state laws and policies, and individual and relational experiences of illegality, highlighting the increasing importance of place for the daily lives and futures of this group.

The Increasing Importance of Place

The legal ecologies of the undocumented young people in this book developed and shifted over time. Starting in the late 1990s and through the early 2000s, the population demographics of both California and Georgia led to divergent approaches to undocumented immigrant inclusion and exclusion. In both locales, even as undocumented young people were being socially integrated into public schools, they witnessed their parents endure exploitative working conditions, fears about driving, and public shaming for their status. These early experiences highlight how Latinx undocumented young adults were developing a sense of precarity and simultaneous legal exclusion and social inclusion long before they graduated from high school. Yet, their childhood experiences also reveal the increasing salience of place for undocumented immigrants.

Southern California's long history as a traditional Latinx immigrant destination created an environment Latinx undocumented young adults described as comforting in many ways. They heard Spanish spoken in their neighborhoods and were surrounded by other Latinxs, contributing to familiarity. The size of the Latinx undocumented immigrant population in Southern California had the paradoxical impact of obscuring the stigma associated with being undocumented, as young people described growing up with relatives and in neighborhoods where many people were also undocumented, rendering status irrelevant in their immediate context at times. Following a tumultuous period in the wake of Proposition 187, an early antecedent of the restrictive state immigration laws like Arizona's Senate Bill (SB) 1070 or Georgia's House Bill (HB) 87, California gradually moved toward inclusion. From 2001, with AB 540, through the 2010s, including expanding financial aid and granting driver's licenses to undocumented immigrants, California has been at the forefront of inclusive state-level policies. Thus, Latinx undocumented young adults in California described much more welcoming day-to-day experiences than Latinx undocumented young adults in Georgia. Despite this trend toward more accommodating state laws, and reflecting their legal ecologies, with no federal immigration solution on the horizon, undocumented young people in the Los Angeles area reported deportation anxiety for their parents and uncertainty about their own long-term plans.

Undocumented young adults living in Atlanta, Georgia, described an increasingly hostile anti-immigrant climate through the late 1990s and into the 2000s, signaling a shift away from the laissez-faire attitude that drew undocumented immigrants to the state. As Georgia emerged as a new immigrant destination, Latinx immigrant enclaves grew in the metropolitan Atlanta area, creating a precarious sense of inclusion. Yet, the racial dynamics of the U.S. South, which had long been focused on a black-white binary, increased the visibility of Latinx undocumented immigrants in the state, in sharp contrast to the experiences of Latinx undocumented young adults in California, echoing the racial politics of visibility (Flores-Gonzales 2017). The intense focus in the late 1990s and through the 2000s on Latinx undocumented immigrants, coupled with restrictive laws and policies, including the Board of Regents ban, sent a clear exclusionary message to Latinx undocumented young adults living in Georgia. The increasingly hostile context not only made life difficult for undocumented young adults but also for their families, which was particularly salient in childhood.

The divergent policy contexts in California and Georgia through the 1990s and 2000s, as reflected in the narratives of Latinx undocumented young adults, reveal how states and localities were increasingly important stakeholders in the immigration debate. Although immigration law is governed at the federal level, laws and policies at the state and local level contribute most directly to the sociopolitical context and, therefore, the day-to-day lives of Latinx undocumented young adults. In their early years, even as they described childhoods that were safe and secure within the context of their families, social forces outside of their families in the form of laws and policies encroached on this safety. As undocumented young people aged into high school, the full effects of inclusionary or exclusionary educational access laws were taking shape. In California, the educational pathways of young people were opening with the introduction of state and institutional financial aid. In contrast, in Georgia, these young people's educational pathways were closed with the passage of Board of Regents policies that cut off educational access.

Educational Access and Belonging

The young adults in this study migrated to the United States between the ages of four months and fifteen years old. School, therefore, was their primary socializing experience. As they moved through the K–12 system, they developed not only the aspiration but also the expectation that they would attend college. This goal was partly informed by the narrative *and* the reality that a college degree is required for social and economic mobility. In both states, young people were deeply motivated by their parents' migration sacrifices. For respondents in Georgia especially, this made their educational exclusion that much more painful. While young people in California were meeting their educational goals, several shared that they had varying levels of support navigating the path to and through college. Some shared that there were college experiences that they were excluded from because of their legal status. This included certain internships, study abroad,[1] and even particular careers. Young people in both states wrestled with the need to alter their educational expectations to adjust to their sociolegal realities. In California, the outcome of these altered educational expectations was not as dire as it was for young people in Georgia because many were enrolled in college and were on a path to graduating. In Georgia, however, the consequences of blocked educational pathways were consequential as the more time young people spent out of college, the more challenging it became to find their way there. Freedom University, a nonprofit educational organization in Georgia,

---

1. DACA recipients can participate in study abroad through Advance Parole, but participants expressed apprehension and uncertainty about the application process and about being able to return.

provided a crucial bridge to college. For those young people who could attend, it kept their hopes of eventually attending college alive through support during the college application process and, perhaps just as important, through a sense of shared community.

While Latinx undocumented young adults were navigating simultaneous inclusion and exclusion for most of their lives, their post–high school educational experiences were particularly consequential for their sense of belonging, in part because of the extended period of social inclusion in school through twelfth grade. Understanding that, for undocumented young people, educational access and a sense of belonging are intimately intertwined reveals a fuller picture of the educational experiences of Latinx undocumented young adults and how this varies across two divergent policy climates. For undocumented young people in Georgia, their forced exit from educational pathways at high school graduation understandably resulted in feelings of disappointment, sadness, and resentment. In California, even though young people could go and were in college, challenges remained for full participation in the typical college experience. The narratives of the young people in this book demonstrate the implicit understanding of the value of a college degree not only as a tool for social mobility but also as a barometer for one's success or failure. For young people in both locales, reaching their full educational potential was integral to honoring their parents' migration sacrifices. This made the barriers they faced that much more consequential for their sense of belonging. Yet, undocumented young people in both California and Georgia demonstrated incredible resilience and agency in the face of exclusionary or incomplete educational experiences.

Advocating for Membership and Full Inclusion

One way that undocumented Latinx undocumented young adults honored their parents' migration sacrifices was by advocating for educational access in their respective locales through activist participation, a form of inclusion as activism (Silver 2018). In the ten years leading up to the publication of this book, the undocumented youth movement has grown, and undocumented youth activists have been at the forefront of the immigrant rights movement. While previous research has focused on undocumented youth activism in contexts like California, understanding the individual pathways into or away from mobilization, beyond welcoming locales like California, is crucial. There was a vibrant movement in Georgia, a testament to the growth and emergence of the undocumented youth movement as a national social movement. As I learned through interviews, activism was just one of several ways for Latinx undocumented young adults to "keep the immigrant bargain." While keeping the immigrant bargain took different forms, including focusing on school, working to contribute to their families, and participating in activism to get an education, respondents in *both* Los Angeles and Atlanta articulated a narrative in which their actions reflected their understanding of honoring their parents' sacrifices, and doing what they can to build better lives for themselves, their families, and future generations.

In both Los Angeles and Atlanta, undocumented young adults were motivated or constrained by varied personal responsibilities and obligations, impacting whether or not they could participate. State contexts shaped Latinx undocumented young adults' perceptions of these obligations. In Los Angeles, where most respondents were enrolled in college, prioritizing their education meant they could become economically self-sufficient and eventually help their parents—the most straightforward understanding of "keeping the immigrant bargain." Young people active in the undocumented youth movement in Georgia held out hope that their activism would change policies in the state and allow them eventually to attend college but also open the door for younger siblings and other undocumented youth in the state. For young people in Georgia who were not actively involved in the undocumented youth movement, working to support their families was yet another way for these immigrant children to fulfill the immigrant bargain. In each of these cases, the intersection of multiple sociolegal contexts shaped the opportunities and actions of Latinx undocumented young adults. Throughout this book, I argue that Latinx undocumented young adults' lives are shaped not only by federal and state laws and policies but also by familial experiences of illegality. By examining participation or nonparticipation in activism among Latinx undocumented young adults, I highlight how state laws and policies intersect with family obligations and educational goals and/or realities to shape undocumented youth mobilization.

Racialized Citizenship and the Ambivalence of Inclusion

In 1903, W. E. B. DuBois described the experience of being African Americans in terms of having a double consciousness or the "sense of always looking at oneself through the eyes of others" (2); additionally, he described his own desire "to make it possible for a man to be both a Negro and an American" (3). The concept of double consciousness is particularly relevant for understanding the experiences of Latinx undocumented young adults because they view themselves through the "eyes" of exclusionary immigration laws *and* racialized narratives about undocumented immigrants. Although they have been characterized in the popular and scholarly discourse as American in every way except on paper, my interviews revealed a complicated relationship with being defined as American and "Americanness" for these young people. Through this work, I explored how the experience of a racialized legal status impacts Latinx undocumented young adults' conceptualizations of Americanness and their understandings of the boundaries, both actual and symbolic, that separate them from American citizens. Latinx undocumented young adults desired to be citizens, both as a pragmatic solution to the uncertainty that permeated their lives and as a form of validation of their lived experience; and they were ambivalent about what it meant to be American.

Their ambivalence revealed the extent to which "American" continues to be primarily associated with whiteness. Latinx undocumented young adults in both California and Georgia who rejected Americanness were conveying their understanding of the racial hierarchy in the United States; this structure clearly placed them outside of the "American" category because of their racial identity *and* their legal status. Those who readily identified as American, however, did so as a way to cognitively assimilate a lifetime lived in the United States and in relation to the idea of returning and living in their home countries—something many of them could not imagine doing. This variation in national and ethnoracial identity development among Latinx undocumented young adults in both California and Georgia is in line with previous research about ethnic identity development among children of immigrants and immigrant children (Rumbaut 2005). Underscoring how identity development processes, especially among immigrant young adults, are not static outcomes; instead, as Rubén Rumbaut (2005) suggests, are "complex products of people's ongoing efforts to interpret, understand, and respond to the social, cultural, historical situations in which they find themselves" (161). For Latinx undocumented young adults in both California and Georgia, the broader federal context of harsh enforcement and deportation policies influences their interpretation of what it means to be American. It also highlights the unique double consciousness of Latinx undocumented young adults as they seek to integrate their identity as noncitizens and racialized subjects *and* their social inclusion in certain aspects of American life.

Ambivalence, as an affective dimension of the experiences of Latinx undocumented young adults, captures the emotional implications of the structural exclusion they experience (Aranda et al. 2015). Further fueling this ambivalence is the temporary nature of DACA, which conferred short-term benefits but maintained long-term uncertainty. DACA also further demonstrated how young adults can experience the same administrative policy differently, depending on where they live. In Georgia, Latinx undocumented young adults were grateful for the benefits of DACA, including getting a driver's license and work permit. Yet DACA also had the unintended consequence of strengthening their connection to the state, as they felt more responsible for their family's safety and well-being due to their protected status. In addition, for many young adults, DACA did not open the door to college as they had hoped. Latinx undocumented young adults in California similarly felt tied to their home state due in part to California's accommodating laws, and connection to their families. While they expressed a desire to leave the state, they did not know what opportunities or restrictions awaited them in other states. Consequently, many planned to stay in California for the foreseeable future.

Latinx undocumented young adults in both states expressed concerns about what the future held for them. Those in California were more optimistic about the future, while Latinx undocumented young adults living in Georgia seemed even more uncertain about what DACA meant for their long-term plans, especially without a college degree. As one participant from California put it, "I'm good *for now*." For the most part,

Latinx undocumented young adults in both regions are living their lives within the boundaries of their liminal legal status; this book suggests that state laws and policies are a key mediating factor but that federal law and policy (or inaction) continue to be powerful forces shaping Latinx undocumented young adults' incorporation pathways and their sense of belonging.

The Incorporation of Latinx Undocumented Young Adults

How immigrants experience integration has long been a question of central concern for immigration scholars. Research demonstrates that the context of reception, primarily through government policies, is a key factor in shaping immigrants' incorporation trajectories (Menjivar 2006; Portes and Rumbaut 2001; Portes and Zhou 1993). In this way, the context of reception serves as a theoretical bridge, enabling this study to consider the precise role of legal status in shaping immigrant inclusion and exclusion. This book contributes to the growing field of studies about the role of legal status in shaping immigrant integration by comparing the experiences of Latinx undocumented young adults in California and Georgia. While previous research about Latinx undocumented young adults focuses almost exclusively on young people living in one locale (Silver 2018; Gonzales 2016; Enriquez 2011; Abrego 2011), this book extends our understanding of the lives of undocumented young people by considering the shared and divergent trajectories of individuals living in very different sociolegal contexts. I conceptualize the complex, dynamic, and shifting social and legal contexts that Latinx undocumented young adults inhabit as their *legal ecologies*. This conceptual framework provides a promising theoretical direction for studying undocumented youth integration because it extends sociological analyses beyond macrolevel factors such as federal immigration laws. While Latinx undocumented young adults in both states readily pointed to their liminal legal status as the main source of their exclusion, they also articulated the influence of both state context *and* their connection to their family on key dimensions of their lives, including their sense of belonging, their educational aspirations, and their participation in activism. These individual, familial, and legal contexts shape the incorporation and mobility opportunities available to Latinx undocumented youth, and these contexts interact to create simultaneous inclusion and exclusion. Conceptualizing these contexts as dimensions of a larger sociolegal ecology broadens our perspective on the integration processes of Latinx undocumented young adults because it accounts for the multiple and sometimes competing influences that shape not only their present-day lives but also their orientations toward their futures, or what seems possible.

This also suggests that there are multiple policy entry points for improving the lives of Latinx undocumented young adults. It was clear from interviews that the most direct and substantive policy solution is a pathway to citizenship—like what the DREAM Act would have accomplished. Undocumented young adults are aware of the unique social position that situates them as "most deserving" of immigration relief. However, as I learned through interviews, undocumented young adults' experiences of illegality are both individual and familial experiences. As such, immigration policy reforms and relief need to include their parents and extended family members. In 2014, President Barack Obama attempted to ease some of the burden of "shared" illegality by proposing the Deferred Action for Parental Arrivals (DAPA) and DACA+ programs. The lengthy legal battle that ensued following the introduction of these programs amplified the continued political and legal vulnerability of the undocumented immigrant population. To the extent that the legal challenge to DAPA and DACA+ was an indication of the larger political climate at the time, Latinx undocumented young adults and their families' fears and uncertainties about trends toward a more hostile national context were realized when Donald Trump ran for president in 2016. Running on an anti-immigrant platform, during his campaign, Trump proposed ending the DACA program. After he was elected in 2016, he followed through on many of his campaign promises related to immigration, including instituting a ban on travel from seven Muslim-majority countries, starting the construction of a wall along the U.S.-Mexico border, and expanding the discretionary power of Immigrations and Customs Enforcement (ICE) officers to detain anyone who, in the judgment of the officers, posed a risk to national security or safety. During this period, gaps between states like California (a welcoming context) and Georgia (a hostile context) widened. California, and other "sanctuary" states, drew the ire of President Trump. In contrast, Georgia, and the Atlanta area in particular, experienced an increase in enforcement. The targeting of immigrant communities in the Atlanta area was so notable that, in 2017, *The New York Times* featured a story detailing the nearly 80 percent increase in immigration arrests made between January and June of that year and quoted the ICE Atlanta Field Office Director stating, "If you're in this country illegally, you should be scared. We're probably going to come knocking at some point."

As many undocumented young people and their families feared, on September 5, 2017, Attorney General Jeff Sessions announced the termination of the DACA program. No new applications would be accepted, and those with DACA would be unable to renew. While the announcement was not a surprise—undocumented young people were aware of Trump's campaign promise to end the program—it was a shock. The end of the program underscored both the value of DACA to undocumented young people and the vulnerability of the program.

Shortly after the program's termination was announced, lawsuits were brought in California, Maryland, New York, and Washington, D.C., challenging the end of the program (National Immigration Law Center 2024). In January 2018, a U.S. District Court in California stopped the termination of the program, allowing recipients with DACA to maintain their status. However, new applications were not being accepted. The challenges to the program's termination eventually made their way to the U.S. Supreme Court, and arguments in the case were heard in November 2018. In June 2020, the Supreme Court held that the termination of DACA was "arbitrary and capricious," reasoning that, in ending the program, the Department of Homeland Security did not offer sufficient reasoning for ending it and did not consider the consequences of ending a program that had benefitted nearly 800,000 recipients, including 650,000 continuous DACA recipients. The Supreme Court decision was a win for DACA holders and their families. Ultimately, the DACA program remains vulnerable to executive administrations that are hostile to immigrant rights. Under the current DACA decision, no new applications are being accepted, leaving many eligible undocumented young people without a way to access the benefits of the DACA program.

Policy Recommendations

The continued legal vulnerability of the DACA program underscores the need for federal immigration reform through a pathway to citizenship for undocumented young people. Yet, this book also reveals that, without a similar pathway to citizenship for undocumented parents, family, and community members, undocumented young adults will continue to share the burden of immigrant illegality. The probability of immigration reform in the current climate is low. Over the course of writing this book, anti-immigrant rhetoric has steadily increased, and immigrants, particularly undocumented Latinx immigrants, have become a target for public outrage. Immigration reform in the form of a pathway to citizenship for undocumented young adults and their families would address legal vulnerabilities; there is deeper work that must be done to address racist nativism, which is on the rise. Yet, there are policy reforms and practices that can be implemented to support undocumented young people and their families.

Beyond federal immigration policy reform, this book highlights the increasingly important role of state laws and policies in facilitating or constraining immigrant inclusion. Many of the benefits of the DACA program for recipients are tied to local and state contexts that mediate the full benefits of the program. The state's power to grant or withhold access to higher education, driver's licenses, and other social benefits profoundly impacts how Latinx undocumented young adults navigate and negotiate their everyday lives. The narratives of undocumented young adults in California show how an inclusive state policy regime can facilitate integration. Access to college, state and institutional financial aid, and professional licenses have opened doors of opportunity. One of the most impactful laws that young people in California noted, however, was driver's licenses for undocumented immigrants, which considerably eased any fears or anxieties they had for their parents, a fear shared by young people in Georgia. Undocumented young people in Georgia were pragmatic about state-level solutions. When asked what, if any, policy they thought would be the most important for undocumented immigrants in the state, their primary recommendation was to allow all undocumented immigrants, not just DACA recipients, to get driver's licenses. Beyond driver's licenses, eliminating the Georgia Board of Regents Policies 4.1.6 and 4.3.4 would align with the spirit and intention of the holding in *Plyler v. Doe* (1982), which was to avoid creating an educational underclass. While the *Plyler* case focused on K–12 education, the value of a college degree in the labor market requires a reconsideration of what we consider necessary education. While both policies should be removed, Policy 4.3.4, requiring that undocumented immigrants pay out-of-state tuition, is the most direct barrier to undocumented students continuing their education in the state of Georgia, a place they consider home.

In addition, this book highlights the role of institutions, like public schools and colleges, in mediating the integration of Latinx undocumented young adults. While this is not a novel finding, in the case of Latinx undocumented young adults living in California, who ostensibly are the most structurally and institutionally included, they continue to experience limitations because of their legal status. High school guidance counselors and teachers should be educated about and understand the legal landscape that impacts undocumented immigrant students, especially as it has shifted dramatically in recent years. The narratives of young people in both California and Georgia show the power of institutional agents to create pivotal moments (Stanton-Salazar 2001; Espinoza 2011) or pathways to college for first-generation students. High schools can ensure that at least one person in the school, whether an administrator, teacher, or counselor, is trained to work with undocumented students to facilitate their college and career goals. This is especially crucial in the current moment, as there are significant threats, legal and administrative, to the DACA program. The legal challenges to DACA have created a new cohort of young people who are DACA-eligible but are unable to apply. In a state like California, these young people are eligible for in-state tuition and state and institutional financial aid. In states like Georgia, they are facing more dire prospects and need more support to navigate the road to college. Key institutional agents are also needed once undocumented young people are in college. As the narratives of collegegoers in California show, if undocumented young people make it to college, there are various extracurricular experiences that may be challenging to navigate, including obtaining internships and research assistantships, and participating in study abroad programs. College administrators and faculty should be aware of ways to support these students' experiential development. Since college is a key point in the transition to adulthood in the United States, Latinx undocumented young adults' exclusion from the experiential aspect of college participation has implications both for their social mobility and for their continued sense of social inclusion or belonging. As more and more undocumented young people enter college without DACA, it is incumbent upon colleges to implement student retention programs and experiences that reflect this reality, starting with developing creative solutions to employ undocumented students on campus. The immigration landscape is shifting rapidly, and college campuses must be innovative and bold in their support of their undocumented immigrant students.

In this book, I focused primarily on high-achieving Latinx undocumented young adults. Yet most young people living in Georgia were not enrolled in college, while all young people in California were either enrolled in college or were college graduates. This demonstrates that, even for high-achieving Latinx undocumented young adults, the barriers to educational success remain high, and the opportunities to fully participate in education and daily life remain limited and, in the current moment, threatened. The Trump administration has promised mass deportations, and it remains to be seen what the full impact of these threats will be. What is certain is that undocumented young people and their families have built their lives in the United States—They are our students, neighbors, and friends. Even as anti-immigrant hostility seeks to other this group, undocumented young people are challenging narratives of blame and are resisting efforts to dehumanize them and their families. While racism, exclusionary nationalism, and white supremacy are deeply entrenched problems in the United States, individuals committed to antiracism, inclusion, and social justice must continue to work together to educate and advocate for a more humane approach to immigration policy and practice in the United States.

WORKS CITED

Abrego, Leisy J. 2006. "'I Can't Go to College Because I Don't Have Papers': Incorporation Patterns of Latino Undocumented Youth." *Latino Studies* 4 (3): 212–31.

Abrego, Leisy J. 2008. "Legitimacy, Social Identity, and the Mobilization of Law: The Effects of Assembly Bill 540 on Undocumented Students in California." *Law and Social Inquiry* 33 (3): 709–34.

Abrego, Leisy J. 2011. "Legal Consciousness of Undocumented Latinos: Fear and Stigma as Barriers to Claims-Making for First- and 1.5-Generation Immigrants." *Law and Society Review* 45 (2): 337–70.

Abrego, Leisy J. 2019. "Relational Legal Consciousness of US Citizenship: Privilege, Responsibility, Guilt, and Love in Latino Mixed-Status Families." *Law and Society Review* 53 (3): 641–70.

Abrego, Leisy J., and Roberto G. Gonzales. 2010. "Blocked paths, uncertain futures: The postsecondary education and labor market prospects of undocumented Latino youth." *Journal of Education for Students Placed at Risk* 15 (1–2): 144–57.

Abrego, Leisy J., and Genevieve Negrón-Gonzales. 2020. *We Are Not Dreamers: Undocumented Scholars Theorize Undocumented Life in the United States.* Duke University Press.

Acevedo-Gil, Nancy. 2017. "College-*Conocimiento*: Toward an Interdisciplinary College Choice Framework for Latinx Students." *Race Ethnicity and Education* 20 (6): 829–50.

Acuna, Rodolfo. 1996. *Anything but Mexican: Chicanos in Contemporary Los Angeles.* Verso Books.

Alba, Richard D., and Victor Nee. 2003. *Remaking the American Mainstream: Assimilation and Contemporary Immigration.* Harvard University Press.

Anderson, Benedict. 2016. *Imagined Communities: Reflections on the Origin and Spread of Nationalism.* Verso.

Aranda, Elizabeth, Elizabeth Vaquera, and Isabel Sousa-Rodriguez. 2015. "Personal and Cultural Trauma and the Ambivalent National Identities of Undocumented Young Adults in the USA." *Journal of Intercultural Studies* 36 (5): 600–19.

Armenta, Amada, and Isabela Alvarez. 2017. "Policing Immigrants or policing immigration? Understanding local law enforcement participation in immigration control." *Sociology Compass* 11 (2): e12453.

Batalova, Jeanne, Sarah Hooker, Randy Capps, and James D. Bachmeier. 2014. *DACA at the Two-Year Mark: A National and State Profile of Youth Eligible and Applying for Deferred Action*. Washington, D.C.: Migration Policy Institute.

Beck, Scott A. L., and Martha Allexsaht-Snider. 2002. "Recent Language Minority Policy in Georgia: Appropriation, Assimilation, and Americanization." In *Education in the New Latino Diaspora*, edited by Stanton Wortham, Enrique J. Murillo, and Edmund T. Hamman. Ablex Publishing.

Bloemraad, Irene, Kim Voss, and Taeku Lee. 2011. "The Protests of 2006: What Were They, How Do We Understand Them, and Where Do We Go?" In *Rallying for Immigrant Rights: The Fight for Inclusion in the 21st Century*, edited by Irene Bloemraad and Kim Voss, 3–43. University of California Press.

Bozick, Robert, Trey Miller, and Matheau Kenashiro. 2016. "Non-citizen Mexican Youth in U.S. Higher Education: A Closer Look at the Relationship Between State Tuition Policies and College Enrollment." *International Migration Review* 50 (4): 864–89.

Browne, Irene, and Mary E. Odem. 2012. "'Juan Crow' in the Nuevo South: Racialization of Guatemalan and Dominican Immigrants in the Atlanta Metro Area." *Du Bois Review: Social Science Research on Race* 9 (2): 321–37.

Bruno, Andorra. 2021. *Deferred Action for Childhood Arrivals (DACA): By the Numbers*. Washington, D.C.: Congressional Research Service. https://www.everycrsreport.com/files/2021-04-14_R46764_7f3a4fbeb56d56e9c24417aaeeb0c27107d03881.pdf.

Burciaga, Edelina M. 2015. "The Promise and Reality of *Plyler v. Doe*: Community Resistance to the School-to-Deportation Pipeline." In *Cracks in the Schoolyard: Confronting Latino Educational Inequality*, edited by Gilberto Q. Conchas and Briana Hinga. Teachers College Press.

Burciaga, Edelina M., and Lisa M. Martinez. 2017. "How Do Political Contexts Shape Undocumented Youth Movements? Evidence from Three Immigrant Destinations." *Mobilization: An International Quarterly*, 22 (4): 178–91.

Burciaga, Edelina M., and Aaron Malone. 2021. "Intensified Liminal Legality: The Impact of the DACA Rescission for Undocumented Young Adults in Colorado." *Law and Social Inquiry* 46 (4): 1092–114.

Burgdofer, Bob. "U.S. Officials Arrest Hundreds of Poultry Workers." Reuters, 2008.

Castles, Stephen, and Alistair Davidson. 2000. *Citizenship and Migration*. Routledge.

Cebulko, Kara. 2014. "Documented, Undocumented, and Liminally Legal: Legal Status During the Transition to Adulthood for 1.5-Generation Brazilian Immigrants." *The Sociological Quarterly* 55 (1):143–67.

Cebulko, Kara, and Alexis Silver. 2016. "Navigating DACA in Hospitable and Hostile States: State Responses and Access to Membership in the Wake of Deferred Action for Childhood Arrivals." *American Behavioral Scientist* 60 (13): 1553–74.

Chacón, Jennifer M. 2012. "Overcriminalizing Immigration." *The Journal of Criminal Law and Criminology* 102 (3): 613–52.

Chavez, Jorge M., and Doris Marie Provine. 2009. "Race and Response of State Legislatures to Unauthorized Immigrants." *The Annals of the American Academy of Political and Social Science* 623 (1): 78–92.

Chavez, Leo. 2008. *The Latino Threat: Constructing Immigrants, Citizens, and the Nation.* Stanford University Press.

Chen, Ming. 2020. *Pursuing Citizenship in the Enforcement Era.* Stanford University Press.

Cheng, Wendy. 2013. *The Changs Next Door to the Diazes.* University of Minnesota Press.

Chishti, Muzaffar, Claire Bergeron, and Kristen McCabe. 2010. *DREAM Act Passes in the House During Lame-Duck Session, But Faces Uphill Battle in Senate.* Washington, D.C.: Migration Policy Institute. https://www.migrationpolicy.org/article/dream-act-passes-house-during-lame-duck-session-faces-uphill-battle-senate.

DeGenova, Nicholas. 2002. "Migrant 'Illegality' and Deportability in Everyday Life." *Annual Review of Anthropology* 31 (1): 419–47.

Dingeman-Cerda, Katie, Edelina M. Burciaga, and Lisa M. Martinez. 2015. "Neither Sinners nor Saints: Complicating the Discourse of Noncitizen Deservingness." *Association of Mexican American Educators* 9 (3): 62–73.

Domina, Thad, AnneMarie Conley, and George Farkas. 2011. "The Link Between Educational Expectations and Effort in the College-for-all Era." *Sociology of Education* 84 (2): 93–112.

DuBois, W. E. B. 1903. *The Souls of Black Folk.* A. C. McClurg & Co.

Durand, Jorge, Douglas S. Massey, and Fernando Charvet. 2000. "The Changing Geography of Mexican Immigration to the United States: 1910–1996." *Social Science Quarterly* 81 (1): 1–15.

Enriquez, Laura E. 2011. "Because We Feel the Pressure and We Also Feel the Support: Examining the Educational Success of Undocumented Immigrant Latina/o Students." *Harvard Educational Review* 81 (3): 476–99.

Enriquez, Laura E. 2015. "Multigenerational Punishment: Shared Experiences of Undocumented Immigration Status Within Mixed-Status Families." *Journal of Marriage and Family* 77 (4): 939–53.

Enriquez, Laura E. 2020. *Of Love and Papers: How Immigration Policy Affects Romance and Family.* University of California Press.

Enriquez, Laura E., and Abigail C. Saguy. 2016. "Coming Out of the Shadows: Harnessing a Cultural Schema to Advance the Undocumented Youth Movement." *American Journal of Cultural Sociology* 4 (1): 107–30.

Espinoza, Roberta. 2011. *Pivotal Moments: How Educators Can Put All Students on the Path to College.* Harvard Education Press.

Faltis, Cristian, and Guadalupe Valdes. 2010. "Educating Immigrant Students, Refugees, and English Language Learners: A No Border Perspective." *Teachers College Record* 112 (14): 285–96.

Faulstich Orellana, Marjorie, Lucia Ek, and Arcelia Hernandez. 1999. "Bilingual Education in an Immigrant Community: Proposition 227 in California." *International Journal of Bilingual Education and Bilingualism* 2 (2): 114–30.

Feliciano, Cynthia. 2009. "Education and Ethnic Identity Formation Among Children of Latin American and Caribbean Immigrants." *Sociological Perspectives* 52 (2): 135–58.

Figueroa, Arina Mangual. 2013. "Citizenship Status and Language Education Policy in an Emerging Latino Community in the United States." *Language Policy* 12: 333–54.

Flores, Stella M. 2010. "State Dream Acts: The Effect of In-State Resident Tuition Policies and Undocumented Latino Students." *The Review of Higher Education* 33 (2): 239–83.

Flores-Gonzales, Nilda. 2017. *Citizens but Not Americans: Race and Belonging Among Latino Millennials*. New York University Press.

Foley, Elise. "Georgia Lawmaker Proposes Driving Cards that Identify 'Illegal Aliens.'" *Huffington Post*, February 9, 2016. Accessed May 7, 2016.

Freedom University. 2021. "Freedom University: History and Timeline." https://www.freedom-university.org/history.

Galindo, Rene. 1997. "Language Wars: Ideological Dimensions of the Debates on Bilingual Education." *Bilingual Research Journal* 21 (2–3): 163–201.

Galindo, Rene. 2012. "Undocumented and Unafraid: The DREAM Act 5 and the Public Disclosure of Undocumented Status as a Political Act." *Urban Review* 44 (5): 589–611.

Garcia, Angela S. 2019. *Legal Passing: Navigating Undocumented Life and Local Immigration Law*. University of California Press.

Gieryn, Thomas F. 2000. "A Space for Place in Sociology." *Annual Review of Sociology* 26: 463–96.

Gleeson, Shannon, and Roberto G. Gonzales. 2012. "When Do Papers Matter? An Institutional Analysis of Undocumented Life in the United States." *International Migration* 50 (4): 1–19.

Glenn, Eveyln Nakano. 2011. "Constructing Citizenship: Exclusion, Subordination, and Resistance." *American Sociological Review* 76 (1): 1–24.

Golash-Boza, Tanya, and Zulema Valdez. 2018. "Nested Contexts of Reception: Undocumented Students at the University of California Central." *Sociological Perspectives* 61 (4): 535–52.

Gonzales, Roberto G. 2008. "Left Out but Not Shut Down: Political Activism and the Undocumented Student Movement." *Northwestern Journal of Law and Social Policy* 3: 219–39.

Gonzales, Roberto G. 2011. "Learning to Be Illegal: Undocumented Youth and Shifting Legal Contexts in the Transition to Adulthood." *American Sociological Review* 76 (4): 602–19.

Gonzales, Roberto G. 2016. *Lives in Limbo: Undocumented and Coming of Age in America*. University of California Press.

Gonzales, Roberto G., Luisa Heredia, and Genevieve Negrón-Gonzales. 2015. "Untangling *Plyler*'s Legacy: Undocumented Students, Schools, and Citizenship." *Harvard Educational Review* 85 (3): 318–41.

Gonzales, Roberto G., Veronica Terriquez, and Stephen P. Ruszczyk. 2014. "Becoming DACAmented: Assessing the Short-Term Benefits of Deferred Action for Childhood Arrivals (DACA)." *American Behavioral Scientist* 58 (14): 1852–72.

Gonzalez, Juan. 2004. *Harvest of Empire: The History of Latinos in America*. Penguin Books.

Gordon, Milton Myron. 1964. *Assimilation in American Life: The Role of Race, Religion, and National Origins*. Oxford University Press.

Goyette, Kimberly 2008. "College for Some to College for All: Social Background, Occupational Expectations, and Educational Expectations Over Time." *Social Science Research* 37: 461–84.

Gutierrez, David. 1995. *Walls and Mirrors: Mexican Americans, Mexican Immigrants, and Politics of Ethnicity*. University of California Press.

Hayes-Bautista, David. 2017. *La Nueva California: Latinos from Pioneers to Post-Millennials*. University of California Press.

HoSang, Daniel Martinez. 2010. *Racial Propositions: Ballot Initiatives and the Making of Postwar California*. University of California Press.

Hochschild, Arlie Russell. 1994. "The Commercial Spirit of Intimate Life and the Abduction of Feminism: Signs from Women's Advice Books." *Theory, Culture, and Society* 11: 1–24.

Hossler, Don, and Karen Syms Gallagher. 1987. "Studying Student College Choice: A Three-Phase Model and the Implications for Policymakers." *College and University* 62 (3): 207–21.

Hurtado, Sylvia, and Deborah Faye Carter. 1997. "Effects of College Transitions and Perceptions of the Campus Racial Climate on Latino College Students' Sense of Belonging." *Sociology of Education* 70 (4): 324–45.

Immigrant Legal Resource Center. April 2022. "Advance Parole for DACA Recipients." https://www.ilrc.org/sites/default/files/resources/advance_parole_for_daca _recipients_april_202261.pdf.

Jimenez, Tomas R. 2008. "Mexican Immigrant Replenishment and the Continuing Significance of Race." *American Journal of Sociology* 113 (6): 152–67.

Jones, Jennifer. 2019. *The Browning of the New South*. The University of Chicago Press.

Jones, Jennifer A. 2012. "Blacks May Be Second Class, but They Can't Make Them Leave: Mexican Racial Formation and Immigrant Status in Winston Salem." *Latino Studies* 10 (1): 60–80.

Jones, Susan R., and Elisa S. Abes. 2013. *Identity Development of College Students: Advancing Frameworks for Multiple Dimensions of Identity*. Jossey Bass.

Kasinitz, Philip, John H. Mollenkopf, Mary C. Waters, and Jennifer Holdaway. 2009. *Inheriting the City: The Children of Immigrants Come of Age*. Russell Sage Foundation Press.

Kaushal, Neeraj. 2008. "In-State Tuition for the Undocumented: Education Effects on Mexican Young Adults." *Journal of Policy Analysis and Management* 27 (4): 771–92.

Lee, Jennifer, and Min Zhou. 2014. "The Success Frame and Achievement Paradox: The Costs and Consequences for Asian Americans." *Race and Social Problems* 6 (1): 38–55.

Lippard, Cameron D. 2011. "Racist Nativism in the 21st Century." *Sociology Compass* 5 (7): 591–606.

Lippard, Cameron D., and Charles A. Gallagher. 2011. *Being Brown in Dixie: Race, Ethnicity, and Latino Immigration in the U.S. South*. First Forum Press.

Louie, Vivian. 2004. *Compelled to Excel: Immigration, Education, and Opportunity Among Chinese Americans*. Stanford University Press.

Louie, Vivian. 2012. *Keeping the Immigrant Bargain: The Costs and Rewards of Success in America*. Russell Sage Foundation.

Marrow, Helen. 2011. *New Destination Dreaming: Immigration, Race, and Legal Status in the Rural American South*. Stanford University Press.

Martinez, Lisa M. 2008. "Flowers from the Same Soil: Latino Solidarity in the Wake of the 2006 Immigrant Mobilizations." *American Behavioral Scientist* 52 (4): 557–79.

Martinez, Lisa M. 2014. "Dreams Deferred: The Impact of Legal Reforms on Undocumented Latino Youth." *American Behavioral Scientist* 58 (14): 1873–90.

McGirr, Lisa. 2001. *Suburban Warriors: The Origins of the New American Right. Politics in Society in Modern American*. Princeton University Press.

Menjivar, Cecilia. 2006. "Liminal Legality: Salvadoran and Guatemalan Immigrants' Lives in the United States." *American Journal of Sociology* 111 (4): 999–1037.

Menjivar, Cecilia, and Leisy Abrego. 2012. "Legal Violence: Immigration Law and the Lives of Central American Immigrants." *American Journal of Sociology* 117 (5): 1380–421.

Migration Policy Institute. 2019. *Unauthorized Immigrant Population Profiles*. https://www.migrationpolicy.org/programs/us-immigration-policy-program-data-hub/unauthorized-immigrant-population-profiles.

Monico, Gabriela. 2020. "American't: Redefining Citizenship in the U.S. Undocumented Immigrant Youth Movement." In *We Are Not Dreamers: Undocumented Scholars Theorize Undocumented Life in the United States*, edited by Leisy J. Abrego and Genevieve Negrón-Gonzales. Duke University Press.

Motomura, Hiroshi. 2014. *Immigration Outside the Law*. Oxford University Press.

Muñoz, Susana. 2015. *Identity, Social Activism, and the Pursuit of Higher Education: The Journey Stories of Undocumented and Unafraid Community Activists*. Peter Lang.

Muñoz, Susana. 2016. "Undocumented and Unafraid: Understanding the Disclosure Management Process for Undocumented College Students and Graduates." *Journal of College Student Development* 57 (6): 715–29.

Muñoz, Susana, and Michelle Espino. 2017. "The Freedom to Learn: Experiences of Students Without Legal Status Attending Freedom University." *The Review of Higher Education* 40 (4): 533–55.

National Conference of State Legislators. 2015. *Report on 2015 State Immigration Laws*. Washington, D.C.: National Conference of State Legislators.

National Conference of State Legislators. 2023. *State Immigration Laws*. Washington, D.C.: National Conference of State Legislators.

National Immigration Law Center. 2024a. *Timeline: DACA in the Courts*. https://www.nilc.org/resources/timeline-daca-in-the-courts/.

National Immigration Law Center. 2024b. *Basic Facts About In-State Tuition for Undocumented Immigrant Students*. https://www.nilc.org/resources/basic-facts -instate/.

Negrón-Gonzales, Genevieve. 2013. "Navigating Illegality: Undocumented Youth and Oppositional Consciousness." *Children and Youth Services Review* 35 (8): 1284–90.

Ngai, Mae. 2004. *Impossible Subjects: Illegal Aliens and the Making of Modern America*. Princeton University Press.

Nicholls, Walter J. 2013. *The DREAMers: How the Undocumented Youth Movement Transformed the Immigrant Rights Debate*. Stanford University Press.

Nicholls, Walter J. 2014. "From Political Opportunities to Niche-Openings: The Dilemmas of Mobilizing for Immigrant Rights in Inhospitable Environments." *Theory and Society* 43 (1): 23–49.

Ochoa, Gilda L. 2004. *Becoming Neighbors in a Mexican American Community: Power, Conflict, and Solidarity*. University of Texas Press.

Odem, Mary E., and Elaine Lacy. 2009. *Latino Immigrants and the Transformation of the U.S. South*. University of Georgia Press.

Olivas, Michael. 2011. *No Undocumented Child Left Behind*: Plyler v. Doe *and the Education of Undocumented Schoolchildren*. New York University Press.

Pabon Lopez, Maria. 2005. "Reflections on Educating Latino and Latina Undocumented Children: Beyond *Plyler v. Doe*." *Seton Hall Law Review* 35: 1373–406.

Pallares, Amalia. 2014. *Family Activism: Immigrant Struggles and the Politics of Noncitizenship*. Rutgers University Press.

Passel, Jeffrey. 2003. *Further Information Relating to the DREAM Act*. Washington, D.C.: The Urban Institute.

Passel, Jeffrey, and D'Vera Cohn. November 2014. *Unauthorized Immigrant Totals Rise in 7 States, Fall in 14: Decline in Those From Mexico Fuels Most State Decreases*. Washington, D.C.: Pew Research Center.

Passel, Jeffrey, and D'Vera Cohn. 2019. *Mexicans Decline to Less Than Half of the U.S. Unauthorized Population for the First Time*. Washington, D.C.: Pew Research Center.

Patler, Caitlin, Jorge A. Cabrera, and Dream Team Los Angeles. 2015. *From Undocumented to DACAmented: Impacts of the Deferred Action for Childhood Arrivals (DACA) Program*. Los Angeles, Calif.: UCLA Institute for Research on Labor and Employment.

Patler, Caitlin, and Roberto G. Gonzales. 2015. "Framing Citizenship: Media Coverage of Anti-Deportation Cases Led by Undocumented Immigrant Youth Organisations." *Journal of Ethnic and Migration Studies* 41 (9): 1453–74.

Perez, Cesar Alesi, Marisol Cuellar Mejia, and Hans Johnson. 2023. *Immigrants in California*. Public Policy Institute of California.

Perez, Patricia, and Patricia McDonough. 2008. "Understanding Latina and Latino College Choice: A Social Capital and Chain Migration Analysis." *Journal of Hispanic Higher Education* 7 (3): 249–65.

Perez Huber, Lindsay, Corina Benavides Lopez, Maria Malagon, Veronica Velez, and Daniel Solorzano. 2008. "Getting Beyond the "Symptom" and Acknowledging the "Disease": Theorizing Racist Nativism." *Contemporary Justice Review* 11 (1): 39–51.

Perna, Laura W. 2006. "Studying College Access and Choice: A Proposed Conceptual Model." In *Higher Education: Handbook of Theory and Research*, edited by John C. Smart, 99–157. Springer.

Phinney, Jean. 1993. "A Three-Stage Model of Ethnic Identity Development in Adolescence." In *Ethnic Identity: Formation and Transmission Among Hispanics and Other Minorities*, edited by Martha E. Bernal and George P. Knight, 61–79. State University of New York Press.

Pitti, Stephen. "The Spirit of Selma: Nine Students Arrested in Georgia for Protesting Discriminatory Education Policies." *Huffington Post*. January 13, 2015. Accessed January 14, 2016.

Portes, Alejandro, Patricia Fernandez-Kelly, and William Haller. 2005. "Segmented Assimilation on the Ground: The New Second Generation in Early Adulthood." *Ethnic and Racial Studies* 28 (6): 1000–40.

Portes, Alejandro, and Rubén Rumbaut. 2001. *Legacies: The Story of the Immigrant Second Generation*. University of California Press.

Portes, Alejandro, and Min Zhou. 1993. "The New Second Generation: Segmented Assimilation and Its Variants." *The Annals of the American Academy of Political and Social Science* 530 (1): 74–96.

Ramakrishnan, Karthick, and Pratheepan Gulasekaram. 2014. *Understanding Immigration Federalism in the United States*. Center for American Progress. https://www.americanprogress.org/article/understanding-immigration-federalism-in-the-united-states/.

Rodriguez, Cassundra. 2018. "Latina/o Citizen Children of Undocumented Parents Negotiating Illegality." *Journal of Marriage and Family* 81 (3): 713–28.

Rodriguez, Cristina. 2008. "The Significance of the Local in Immigration Reform." *Michigan Law Review* 106 (4): 567–942.

Rodriguez, Cristina, Chishti Muzaffar, and Kimberly Nortman. 2010. "Legal Limits on Immigration Federalism." In *Taking Local Control: Immigration Policy Activism in U.S. Cities and States*, edited by Monica W. Varsanyi, 32–50. Stanford University Press.

Rodriguez Vega, Silvia. 2018. "Borders and Badges: Arizona's Children Confront Detention and Deportation Through Art." *Latino Studies* 16: 310–40.

Rosa, Jonathan, and Nelson Flores. 2017. "Unsettling Race and Language: Toward a Raciolinguistic Perspective." *Language in Society* 46 (5): 621–47.

Rosales, Jesenia. 2024. "Latinx Undocumented Students College Choice." *Journal of Latinos and Education* 23 (1): 193–204.

Rosenbaum, James. 2001. *Beyond College for All: Career Paths for the Forgotten Half.* Russell Sage Foundation.

Rumbaut, Rubén. 1994. "The Crucible Within: Ethnic Identity, Self-Esteem, and Segmented Assimilation Among Children of Immigrants." *International Migration Review* 28 (4): 748–94.

Rumbaut, Rubén. 2008. "Reaping What You Sow: Immigration, Youth, and Reactive Ethnicity." *Applied Developmental Science* 12 (2): 108–11.

Rumbaut, Rubén G. 2005. "Sites of Belonging: Acculturation, Discrimination and Ethnic Identity Among Children of Immigrants." In *Discovering Successful Pathways in Children's Development: Mixed Methods in the Study of Childhood and Family Life*, edited by Thomas S. Weisner, 111–162. The University of Chicago Press.

Santa-Ramirez, Stephen. 2022. "A Sense of Belonging: The People and Counterspaces Latinx Undocumented/DACA Students Use to Persist." *Education Sciences* 12 (10): 691–707.

Schrag, Peter. 2010. *Not Fit for Our Society: Immigration and Nativism in America.* University of California Press.

Seginer, Rachel. 2008. "Future Orientation in Times of Threat and Challenge: How Resilient Adolescents Construct Their Future." *International Journal of Behavioral Development* 32 (4): 272–82.

Seif, Hinda. 2004. "'Wise Up!': Undocumented Latino Youth, Mexican-American Legislators, and the Struggle for Higher Education Access." *Latino Studies* 2: 210–30.

Seif, Hinda. 2011. "'Unapologetic and Unafraid': Immigrant Youth Come Out From the Shadows." *New Directions for Child and Adolescent Development* 134: 59–75.

Silver, Alexis. 2018. *Shifting Boundaries: Immigrant Youth Negotiating National, State, and Small-Town Politics.* Stanford University Press.

Singer, Audrey. 2004. "The Rise of New Immigrant Gateways." Chicago, Ill.: Financial Access for Immigrants Conference: Learning from Diverse Perspectives.

Singer, Audrey, Susan W. Hardwick, and Caroline B. Brettell, eds. 2008. *21st Century Gateways: Immigrant Incorporation in Suburban America.* Washington, D.C.: The Brookings Institution.

Smith, Robert Courtney. 2006. *Mexican New York: Transnational Lives of New Immigrants.* University of California Press.

Soltis, Laura Emiko. 2015. "From Freedom Schools to Freedom University: Liberatory Education, Interracial and Intergenerational Dialogue, and the Undocumented Student Movement in the U.S. South." *Souls: A Critical Journal of Black Politics, Culture, and Society* 17 (1–2): 20–53.

Stanton-Salazar, Ricardo. 2001. *Manufacturing Hope and Despair: The School and Kin Support Networks of US-Mexican Youth.* Teachers College Press.

Stuesse, Angela. 2016. *Scratching Out a Living: Latinos, Race, and Work in the Deep South.* University of California Press.

Stuesse, Angela, and Mathew Coleman. 2014. "Automobility, Immobility, Altermobility: Surviving and Resisting the Intensification of Immigrant Policing." *City and Society* 26 (1): 51–72.

Suárez-Orozco, Carola, Hirokazu Yoshikawa, Robert T. Teranishi, and Marcelo M. Suárez-Orozco. 2011. "Growing Up in the Shadows: The Developmental Implications of Unauthorized Status." *Harvard Educational Review* 81 (3): 438–73.

Svajlenka, Nicole Prchal, and Audrey Singer. 2013. *Immigration Facts: Deferred Action for Childhood Arrivals*. Washington, D.C.: Brookings Institution. https://www.brookings.edu/articles/immigration-facts-deferred-action-for-childhood-arrivals-daca/.

Terriquez, Veronica. 2015. "Intersectional Mobilization, Social Movement Spillover, and Queer Youth Leadership in the Immigrant Rights Movement." *Social Problems* 62 (3): 343–62.

Tovar, Jessica, and Cynthia Feliciano. 2009. "'Not Mexican-American, but Mexican': Shifting Ethnic Self-Identities Among Children of Mexican Immigrants." *Latino Studies* 7 (2): 197–221.

Trivette, Michael J., and David J. English. 2017. "Finding Freedom: Facilitating Postsecondary Pathways for Undocumented Students." *Educational Policy* 31 (6): 858–94.

Unzueta Carrasco, Tania A., and Hinda Seif. 2014. "Disrupting the Dream: Undocumented Youth Reframe Citizenship and Deportability Through Anti-Deportation Activism." *Latino Studies* 12 (2): 279–99.

Valadez Torres, Martin. 2005. "Indispensable Migrants: Mexican Workers and the Making of Twentieth-Century Los Angeles." In *Latino LA: Transformations, Communities, and Activism*, edited by Enrique Ochoa and Gilda L. Ochoa. The University of Arizona Press.

Vargas, Jose Antonio. 2011. "My Life as an Undocumented Immigrant." *New York Times*, 2011, Sunday Magazine.

Varsanyi, Monica. 2010. *Taking Local Control: Immigration Policy Activism in the U.S. Cities and States*. Stanford University Press.

Wainer, Andrew. 2006. "The New Latino South and the Challenge of American Public Education." *International Migration* 44 (5): 129–65.

Walker, Kyle E., and Helga Leitner. 2011. "The Variegated Landscape of Local Immigration Policies in the United States." *Urban Geography* 32 (2): 156–78.

Weeks, Gregory B., and John R. Weeks. 2010. *Irresistible Forces: Explaining Latin American Migration to the United States and Its Effects on the South*. University of New Mexico Press.

Weise, Julie 2015. *Corazon de Dixie: Mexicanos in the U.S. South Since 1910*. The University of North Carolina Press.

Wickert, David. 2016. "How the Olympics Helped Lure Latinos to Atlanta." *The Atlanta Journal-Constitution*, July 15, 2016.

Wong, Kent, Jann Shadduck-Hernandez, Fabiola Inunza, Julie Monroe, Victor Narrio, and Abel Valenzuela Jr. 2012. *Undocumented and Unafraid: Tam Tran, Cinthya Felix, and the Immigrant Youth Movement*. Los Angeles, Calif.: UCLA Labor Center.

Wong, Tom K., Kelly K. Richter, Ignacia Rodriguez, and Philip E. Wolgin. 2015. *Results from a Nationwide Survey of DACA Recipients Illustrate Program's Impact.* Center for American Progress. https://www.americanprogress.org/article/results-from-a-nationwide-survey-of-daca-recipients-illustrate-the-programs-impact/.

Wong, Tom K., Ignacia Rodriguez Kmec, Diana Pliego, Karen Fierro Ruiz, Silva Mathema, Trinh Q. Truong, Rosa Barrientos-Ferrer. 2024. *Results from 2024 National DACA Study.* Center for American Progress. https://www.americanprogress.org/article/2023-survey-of-daca-recipients-highlights-economic-advancement-continued-uncertainty-amid-legal-limbo/.

Wong, Tom K., and Carolina Valdivia. 2014. *In Their Own Words: A Nationwide Survey of Undocumented Millennials.* San Diego, Calif.: Center for Comparative Immigration Studies.

Yoshikawa, Hirokazu. 2011. *Immigrants Raising Citizens: Undocumented Parents and Their Children.* Russell Sage Foundation.

Yosso, Tara J. "Whose Culture Has Capital? A Critical Race Theory Discussion of Community Cultural Wealth." *Race Ethnicity and Education* 8 (1): 69–91.

Yuval-Davis, Nira. 2006. "Belonging and the Politics of Belonging." *Patterns of Prejudice* 40 (3): 197–214.

Zepeda-Millan, Chris. 2017. *Latino Mass Mobilization: Immigration, Racialization, and Activism.* Cambridge University Press.

Zolberg, Aristide R. 2006. *A Nation by Design: Immigration Policy in the Fashioning of America.* Russell Sage Foundation.

Zong, Jie, and Jeanne Batalova. 2019. *How Many Unauthorized Immigrants Graduate from U.S. High Schools.* Washington, D.C.: Migration Policy Institute.

Zuniga, Victor, and Ruben Hernandez-Leon. 2009. "The Dalton Story: Mexican Immigration and Social Transformation in the Carpet Capital of the World." In *Latino Immigrants and the Transformation of the U.S. South,* edited by Mary E. Odem and Elaine Lacy. University of Georgia Press.

INDEX

Page numbers for tables, figures, and illustrations are in **bold**. *Italicized* words indicate words italicized in the text.

ABOUT THE AUTHOR

Edelina M. Burciaga is an assistant professor of sociology at the University of Colorado, Denver. Her research focuses on undocumented Latinx youth in the United States, examining how state and local laws shape their transition into adulthood. She has conducted studies in California, Georgia, and Colorado. Burciaga's work has been published in several academic journals, contributing to the understanding of the experiences and challenges faced by undocumented immigrant young people in the United States.